AF251412

The Bolivar Point Lighthouse

Reflections of the historic lighthouse
from those who call this peninsula home.

By
Denise Adams
and
Russell Autrey

Bolivar Light Publishing
Russell Autrey
P.O. Box 145
Port Bolivar, TX 77650

Copyright © 2022 by Russell Autrey
All rights reserved.

Remembrances
of the
Bolivar Point Lighthouse

No part of this book may be scanned, reproduced, distributed or transmitted in any form or by any means including photocopying, recording or by any electronic methods without the express permission of the publisher, except in case of brief quotations embodied in critical reviews and certain other non-commercial uses permitted by U.S. Copyright laws. For other permission requests, contact the publisher below.

The Bolivar Point Lighthouse © 2022, Bolivar Light Publishing, Russell Autrey

First Edition: January, 2022

Bolivar Light Publishing
Russell Autrey
P.O. Box 145
Port Bolivar, Texas 77650

Publisher's Catalog In-Publication Data:

Names: Adams, Denise | Autrey, Russell
Title: The Bolivar Point Lighthouse
Illustrations: Autrey, Russell
Description: Lighthouse | Preservation | Personal stories | Photographs

Library of Congress Number: 2021923807

ISBN: 978-1-7363130-0-8

All Rights Reserved.

Subjects: Lighthouse History | Recollections | Photographs | Preservation

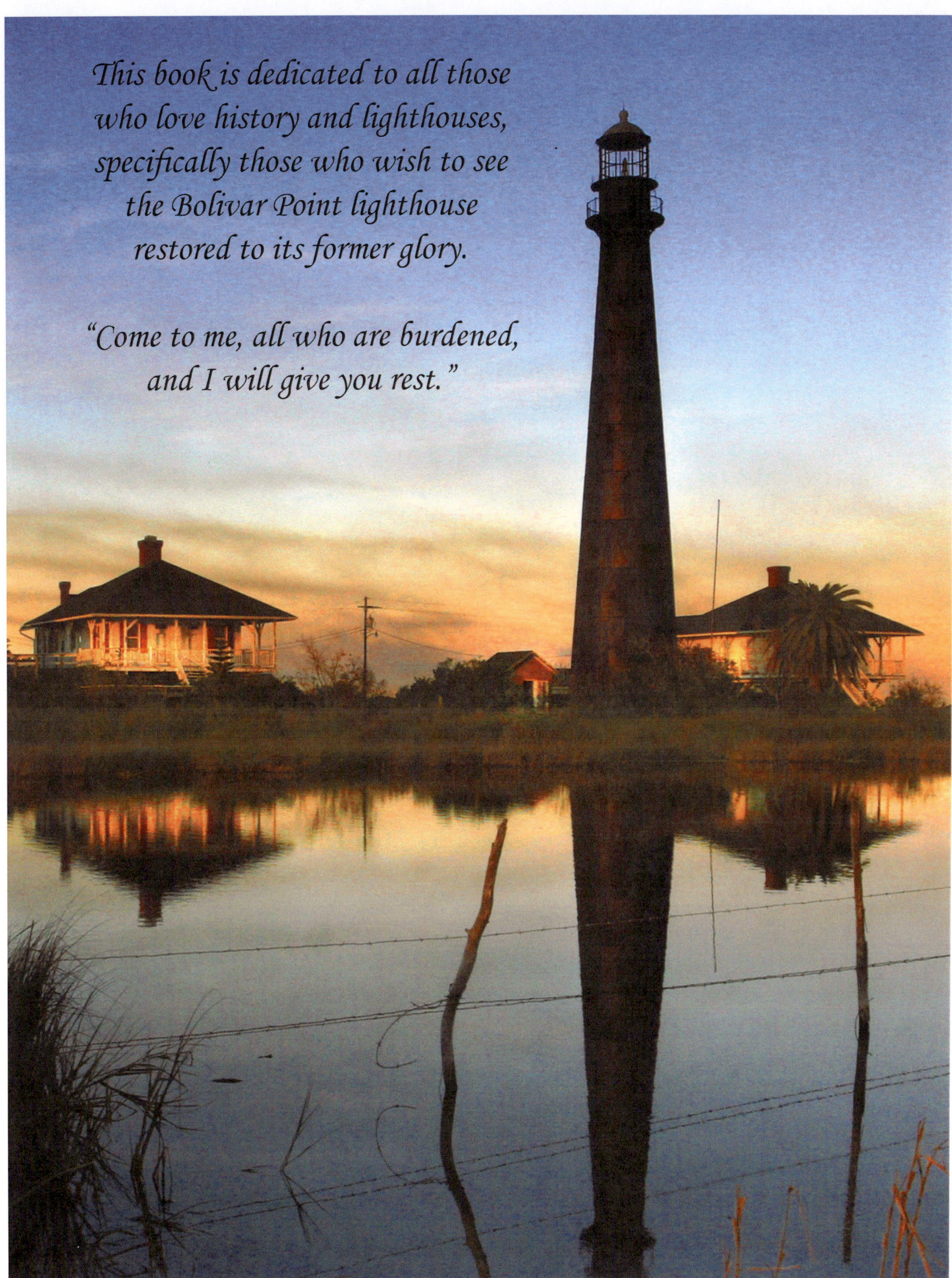
This book is dedicated to all those
who love history and lighthouses,
specifically those who wish to see
the Bolivar Point lighthouse
restored to its former glory.

"Come to me, all who are burdened,
and I will give you rest."

The Mission - Save the Lighthouse

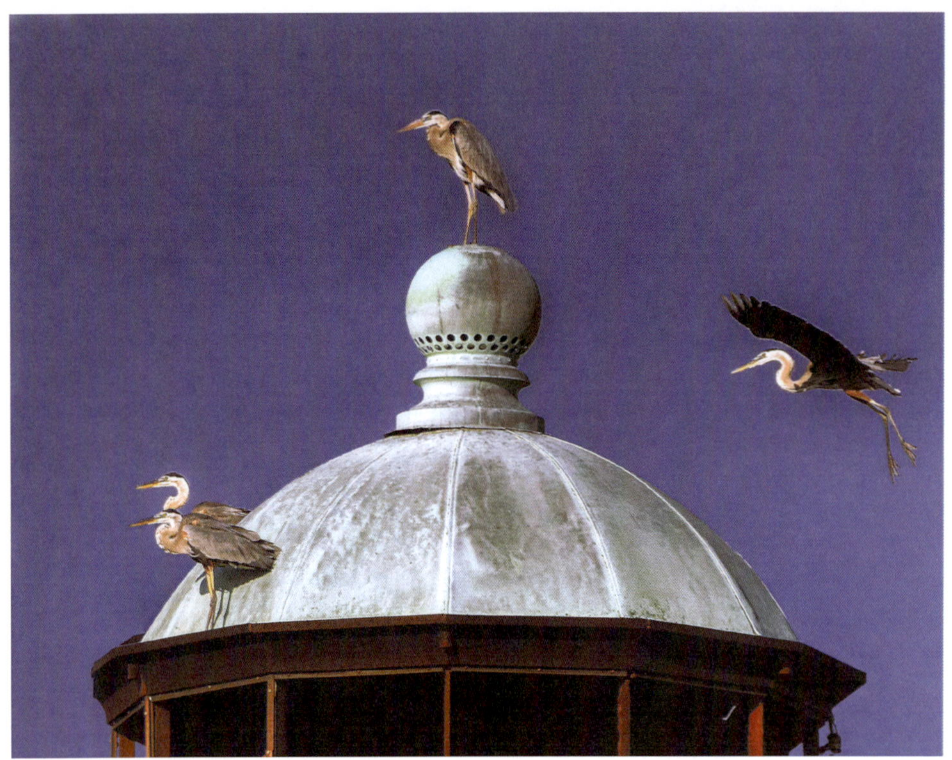

The Bolivar Point Lighthouse has been standing guard over the peninsula since 1872. The lighthouse has survived numerous hurricanes, including the devastating 1900 storm, as well as hurricanes Alicia, Carla and Ike.

Sadly, like many historic sites, the years have taken their toll on this grand dame. Our goal is to help with the preservation and restoration of the lighthouse for this and future generations.

Proceeds from the sale of this book will benefit the lighthouse preservation fund, and all photos and writings were donated. Many thanks to those generous residents and fans of the lighthouse who shared their memories, and the memories of their families, to make this labor of love a reality.

All photos were taken by award-winning Texas photographer and illustrator Russell Autrey over a five-year span. His outstanding photographs have appeared in magazines and Texas newspapers, especially over his 30-year career with The Herald-Coaster, now The Fort Bend Herald, a daily newspaper in Rosenberg. Autrey has published numerous coffee-table and children's' books, and his drawings and photos have been featured in numerous exhibits. Personal narratives were collected by Denise Adams, an award-winning journalist and writer.

The lighthouse is a vital part of Texas history and is in danger of being past the point of reconstruction. She deserves to be restored and remembered, and your donations and the purchase of this book will help make that dream a reality.

As so many of the residents in this book have stated, "the lighthouse belongs to all of us." Let's keep this grand dame standing tall and proud in the manner in which she deserves after so many years of service to the Texas coast and the many sailors who looked to her for a port in the storm.

- Russell and Denise

Memories from Amy Maxwell Chase

The lighthouse is magical.

As a little girl, I can remember sitting in the car, coming down Highway 87. The lighthouse looked so small from far away. The first one to spot it won. There was giddy excitement as we got closer. I couldn't sleep the night before…counting the hours until we'd be on the road headed to Bolivar. Pulling up, there was a magnitude to the lighthouse that was spectacular.

In the 1980's, when I'd climb up to the top….I'd sit and watch for pelicans. The pelicans were almost extinct back then. I would just hope to see one fly by…but I can remember sitting up there just staring at the unobstructed view for miles on end.

We had a site visit from our historical architect. The door to the lighthouse was open, and it was about 1 in the morning. I needed to lock it up. People have said the lighthouse was haunted. I walked in there, and it was like it was calling my name. I sat on the staircase for 30 minutes and prayed. I felt a peaceful warmth and there was nothing scary. Before then, I was scared to go in there by myself, especially at night. But that night was different. It was so peaceful as I sat thinking of the rich Texas history of what the lighthouse has meant to so many and the hundreds of lives that had been spared by riding out hurricanes.

It is such an honor to be heading up the Foundation. In 2015, Michael, my cousin, created the Bolivar Point Lighthouse Foundation, a 501(c)(3) non-profit organization to have the lighthouse restored. He did an amazing job getting the project started. Earlier this year, I left my corporate career after 22 years to head up the Foundation. It is an honor to be in this role.

This is the project of a lifetime. Everyone wants to help. God has put amazing people in our lives, and we're constantly meeting wonderful new people.

We have a fabulous historical architect. I actually met him on a Southwest flight three years ago flying from Amarillo to Austin when he sat next to me…definitely serendipitous. We are blessed to have him working on our project. Our goal is that one day the lighthouse will be open to the public in a controlled manner and we'll have educational programs.

Jane Long, the Mother of Texas, lived here and the lighthouse has survived many storms including the 1900 and 1915 storms and Hurricane Ike. The lighthouse is here because of Galveston and the Ship Channel. There are people who are lighthouse lovers from all over the US who email, asking if it is open to the public. Tourists drive to the back gate or sit off 87 and take pictures or paint the lighthouse daily. It is heartwarming to see how much love there is for this iconic landmark.

I took our daughters to Washington D.C. to see the Fresnel Lens from the Bolivar Point Lighthouse for the first time. They were just mesmerized. The series of lenses and prisms in the shape of a beehive are absolutely stunning and gorgeous. You could just sit and stare at its beauty for hours.

The lighthouse welcomes you. It's the first and the last thing people see entering or leaving the peninsula. The lighthouse is a significant piece of Texas history and absolutely deserves to be restored. This is a Stewardship mission.

> "The lighthouse is the anchor of the peninsula and deserves to be restored."

To help restore and preserve the Bolivar Peninsula Lighthouse, contact the non-profit Bolivar Point Lighthouse Foundation at P. O. Box 385, Port Bolivar, TX 77650 or follow them on Facebook.

A Brief History of the Lighthouse

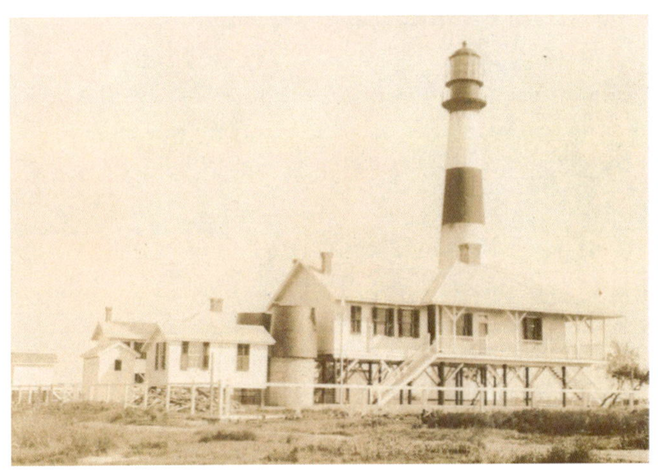

On July 15, 1870, Congress appropriated $40,000 for an iron lighthouse on Bolivar Point. The brick lighthouse, which stands 117 feet above sea level, is sheathed in cast-iron plates riveted together, and anchored to a nine-foot concrete foundation. It was originally painted with black and white horizontal bands to provide a distinctive day-mark.

The new lighthouse opened in 1872. The 52,000 candle-powered beacon guided ships safely from the Gulf of Mexico, through the channel, and into Galveston's harbor. The burner of the lamp was fed by kerosene, contained in storage tanks on the lower level. The kerosene was forced through nozzles into a mantle where it became gas, burning with great intensity. Eight rays of light were produced every 15 seconds as the lamp slowly revolved throughout the night. The lighthouse has withstood the onslaught of some of the worst storms recorded on the Texas Gulf Coast. During the 1900 storm, 125 people sought shelter in the lighthouse, huddling on the iron-steps to escape the storm surge. Sixty-one people found safety on the lighthouse steps during the hurricane in 1915. The lighthouse was officially retired in 1933, when the South Jetty lighthouse replaced it. The inner mechanisms, lamps and reflectors- which burned with the power of 52,000 candles- were disassembled. The lighthouse's lens was reassembled and is on display at the Smithsonian's National Museum of American History in Washington, DC.

- Information courtesy of the Galveston Historical Foundation

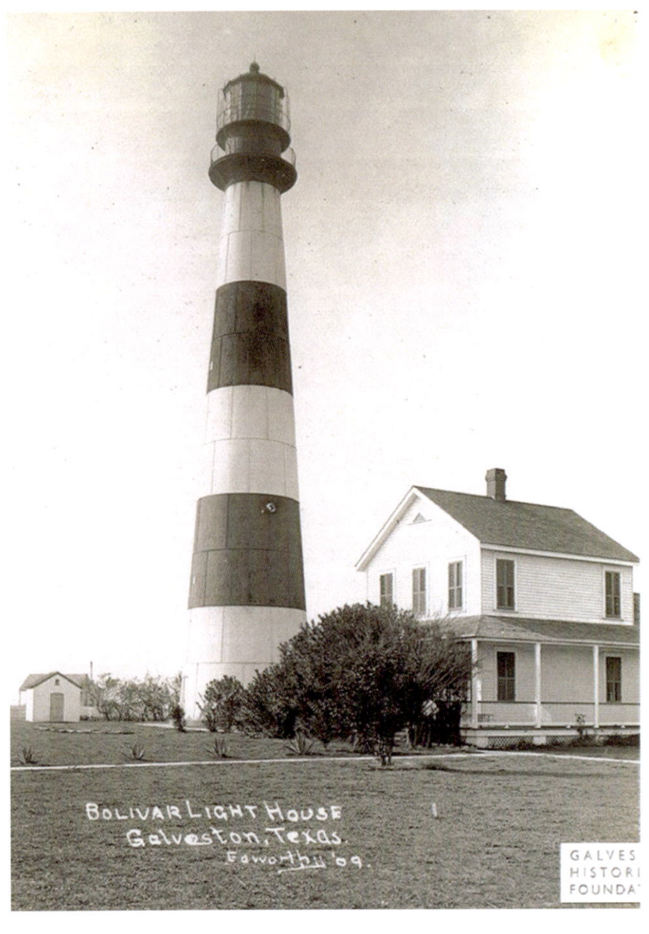

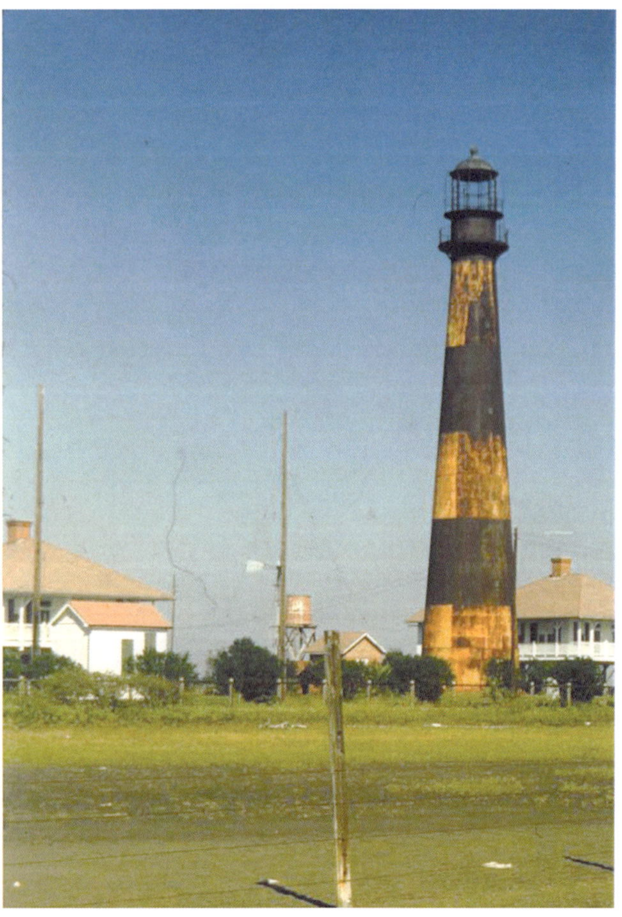

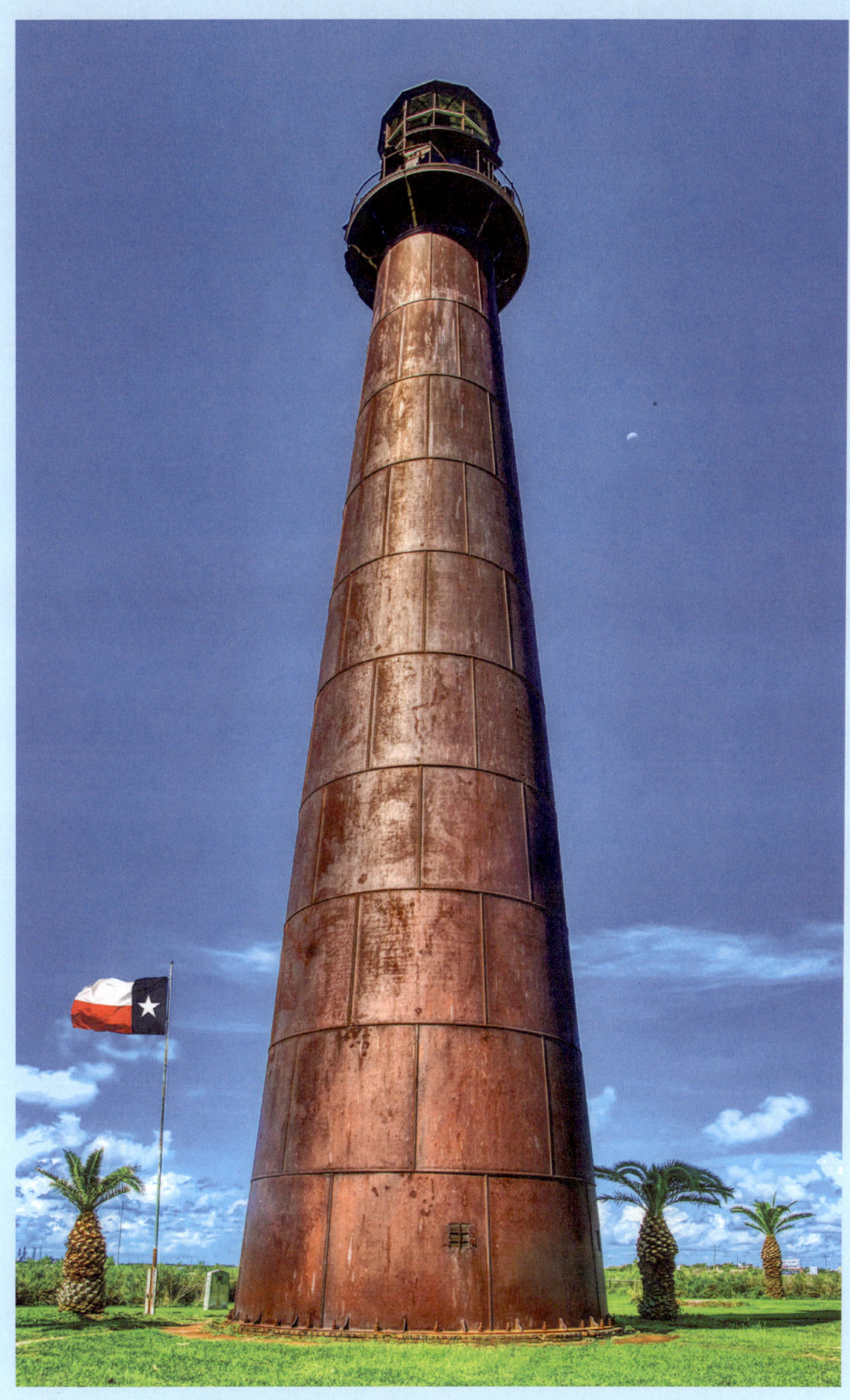

'Our ancestors, a family of five, survived the 1900 storm sitting on the steps in the lighthouse with 120 others.'

Memories from Linda Adams

"William Henry Mellen and Marie Elisee Lizzie Mellen came to Texas by way of Lafayette, Louisiana. William Henry was an itinerant worker and came to Texas during the oil boom.

They had eight children before the 1900 Storm. However, three died, leaving five alive at the time of the storm. Helena Pearl was 13, Grenville Stanford was 12, Marie Evadne ("Beebe") was 8, Leona Lucille was 4, and Lizzie Ada (Elizabeth Callista a/k/a MeMe) was 3.

Aunt Shirley Fivel Bradley told me that Helena Pearl and Grenville were going to school in Galveston and were not allowed to return home when the storm hit.

The teachers, nuns, at the two Catholic schools kept them safe and probably saved many lives. Shirley said that William Henry came home that evening and said a storm was coming so they got the goats and chickens up on the porch.

As the storm intensified, it was decided to go to the lighthouse. He swam MeMe on his back and they were the last to get inside before the storm surge raised the water up over the door frame. Our ancestors, a family of five, survived the 1900 Storm sitting on the 180+ steps in the lighthouse with 120 others.

MeMe told Roland, her great-grandson, and some of the family, that the screams from those trying to get inside the lighthouse to safety could be heard but H.C. Claiborne, the lighthouse keeper, couldn't open the door because the lighthouse would've flooded. He and his wife helped the survivors during and after the storm.

William Henry was 41 and Marie Elise was 33 at the time of the 1900 Storm. My grandmother, MeMe, said she had nightmares about so many crying to let them in.

William Henry and Marie Elisee went on to have four more children. Earl Mellen died in childbirth in 1901. Marie Elisee died in 1921 and William Henry died in 1925."

- Linda Adams, age 76

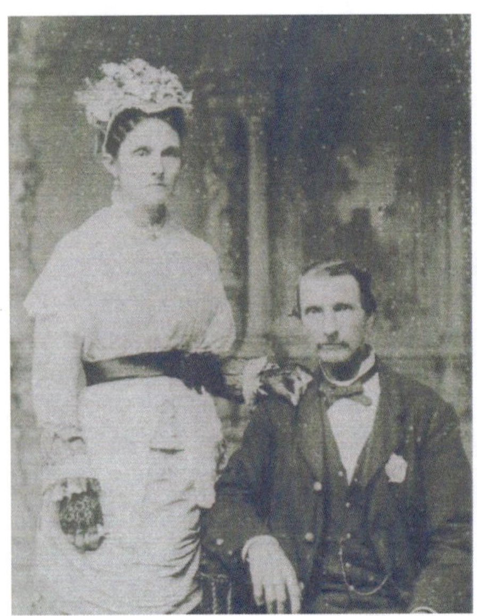
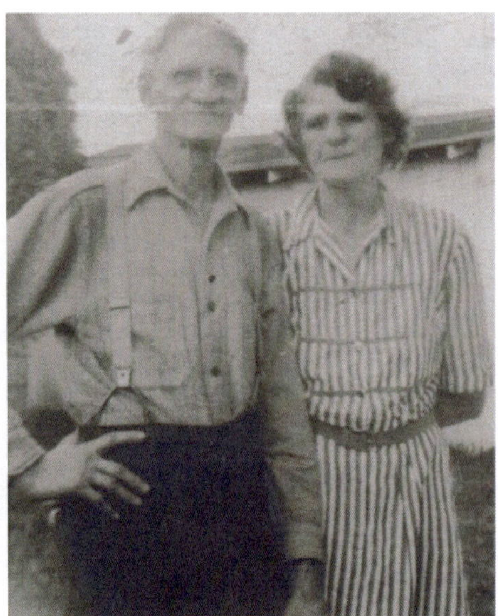
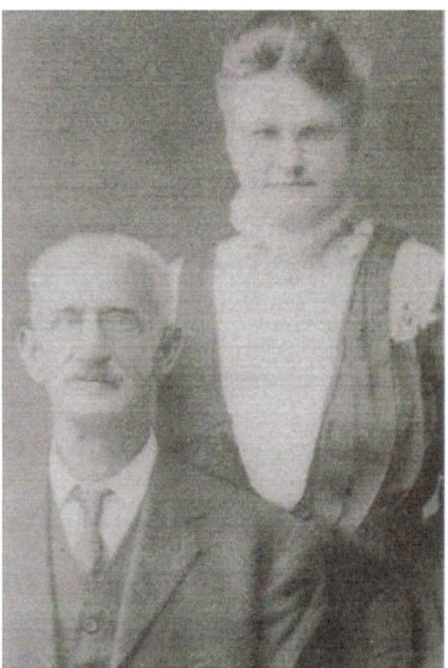

"William Henry Mellen and Marie Elisee Mellen were my great grandparents. Elizabeth Callista Mellen was my grandmother. Shirley Fivel Bradley is my grandmother's youngest child. Roland Adams (my son) is her great grandson." - Linda Adams

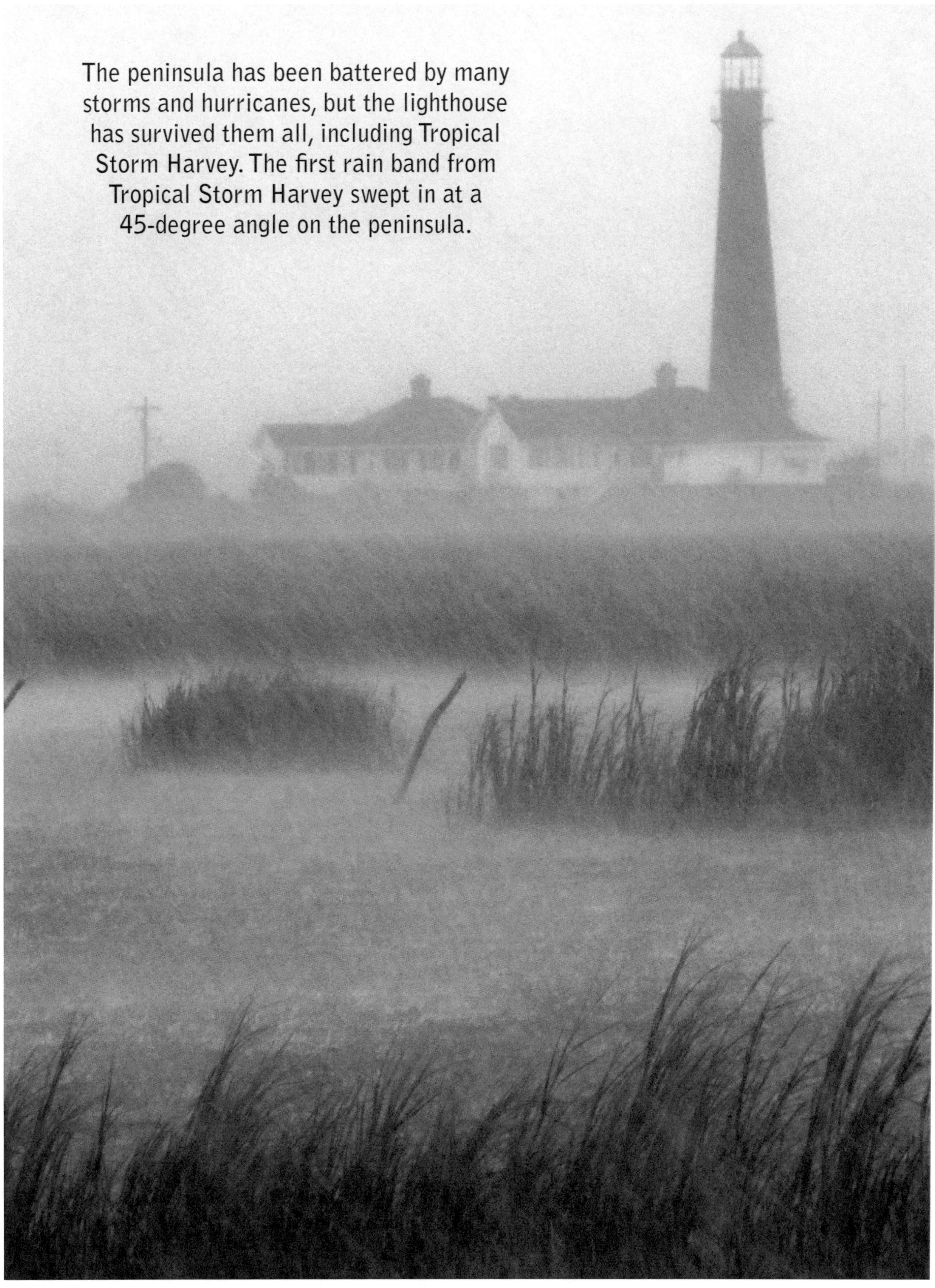

The peninsula has been battered by many storms and hurricanes, but the lighthouse has survived them all, including Tropical Storm Harvey. The first rain band from Tropical Storm Harvey swept in at a 45-degree angle on the peninsula.

The Devastating 1900 Hurricane

A typed transcript of Eleanor Whittington's letter can be found on Pag11 7. She was the granddaughter of Oliver Howard Bassett.

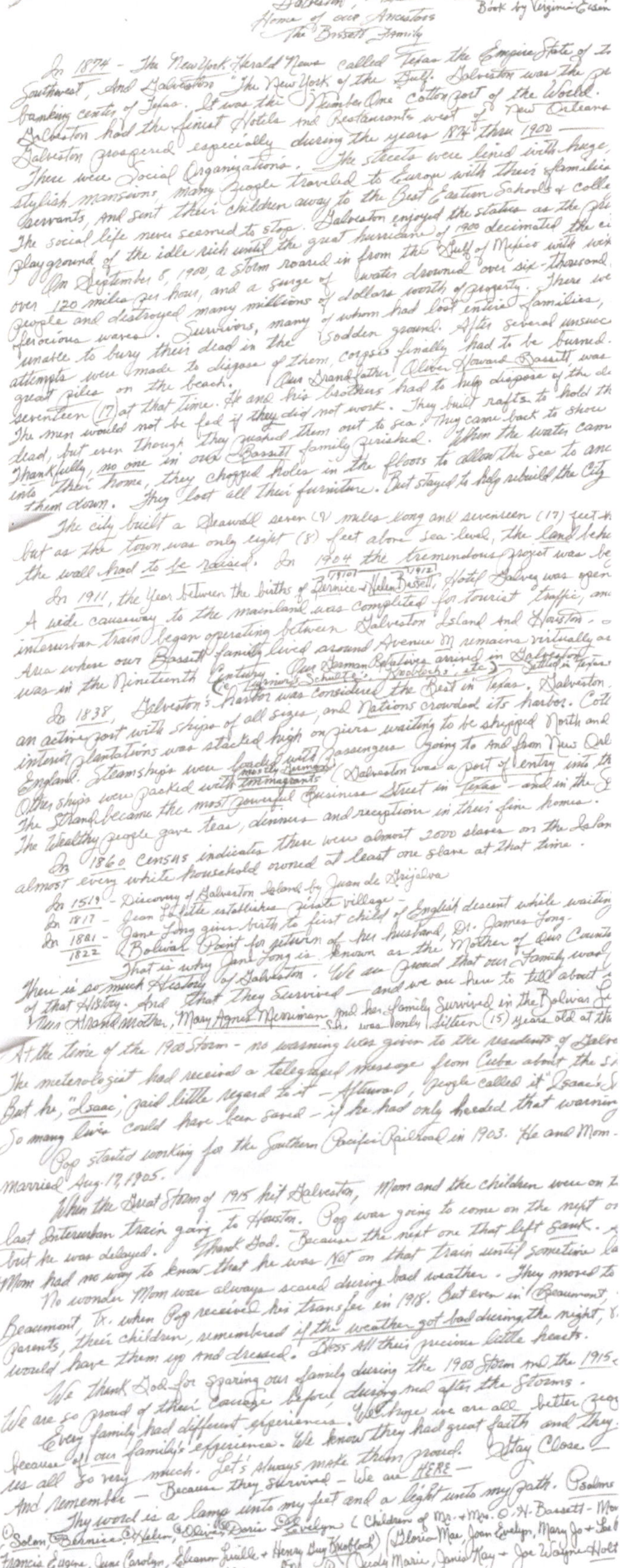

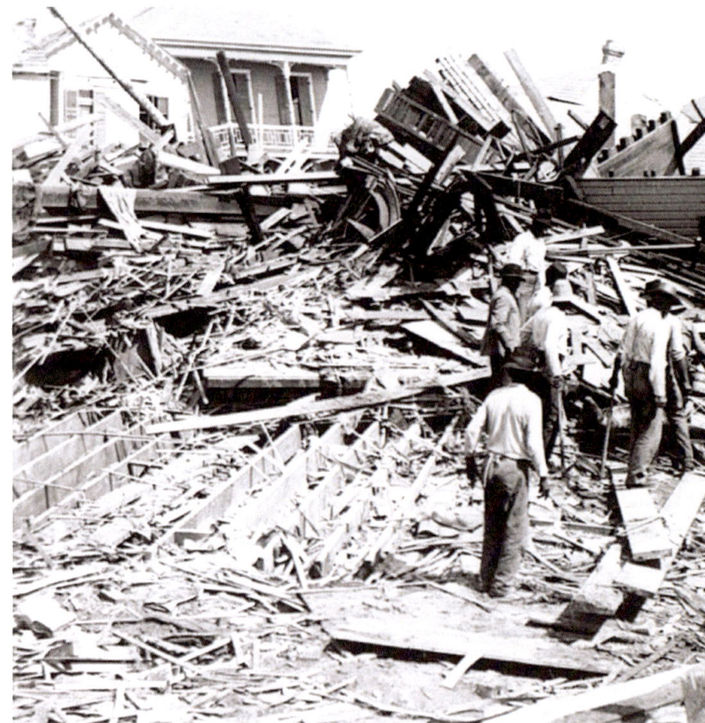

Galveston after the storm.

BER 10, 1900.

MONDAY'S WORK.

Able-Bodied Men Who Refuse to Work Will Not Be Fed.

Galveston, Monday.

A second meeting of the relief committee was held Monday morning, with Chairman W. A. McVitie presiding, and Messrs. W. C. Ogilvy and Chrales L. Dorsey as secretaries.

The question of removing debris from the streets was discussed at considerable length. It was reported that it was difficult to get men to work at clearing away the debris. A great deal of looting has been going on, and others who have not indulged in this prectice have gotten supplies from the relief committee without working.

Mr J. H. Hawley spoke pretty warmly upon this matter, and said no able-bodied man who refuses to work should be given food.

Chief-of-Police Ketchum, who arrived on the scene at this moment, said that the committee should seize all food supplies in the city at once—should notify every wholesale grocery and the flour mills that all the food they had on hand belonged to the committee and would be paid for by it. Then the committee should take charge of the distribution of these supplies, and should permit no able-bodied man to eat unless he worked.

Mr. Hawley said the city should be placed under martial law and all food supplies should be guarded.

A messenger was dispatched to notify the wholesale grocers and the flour mills that the committee had taken charge of all their food supplies.

On motion of Mr Forster Rose it was ordered that the chairman of each ward should have charge of the removal of debris in his ward, and should have charge of the food supplies for that ward...

(adjacent column)

...d the committee ... all the money im-

...MITTEE.

...ief committee was ...vening, Mr. W. A. ...siding. W. C. Ogil- ... of the meeting.

...ster Rose, the chair- ...employ a permanent ... the week.

...sted that the city be ...ll of the committee ...irman be elected for ...s done, and the fol- ...n, to have charge of ...ir respective districts

...homas Doyle.
Chas. L. Wallis.
Jake Davis.
A. C Torbett.
C. H. McMaster.
George Stenzel.
...r. Forster Rose.
...t. Edmond Bourke.
...Clrarence Ousley.
...W. F Coakley.
...Mr. John Goggan.
Mr. Edgar J. Berry.

...mittee for the different ...wered and instructed to ...elief wherever necessary. ...have been appointed by ...le as purchasing commit- ...llis, Jake Davis. M. Ull- ...sing, Gus Lewy and H. C. ...orsey has been appointed

...COMMITTEES.

Bringing Order Out of ...haos Begun.

A newspaper article published in Galveston after the devastating 1900 hurricane.

Galveston, Texas
House of Our Ancestors
The Bassett Family - Written by
Eleanor Whittington, granddaughter of
Oliver Howard Bassett

In 1874 - The New York Herald News called Texas the Empire State of the Southwest and Galveston "The New York of the Gulf." Galveston was the banking center of Texas. It was the "Number One" cotton port of the World. Galveston had the finest hotels and restaurants west of New Orleans. Galveston prospered, especially during the years 1874 through 1900. There were Social Organizations. The streets were lined with huge stylish mansions. Many people traveled to Europe with their families and servants and sent their children away to the Best Eastern Schools and colleges. The social life never seemed to stop. Galveston enjoyed the status as the private playground of the idle rich until the great hurricane of 1900 decimated the city.

On September 8, 1900, a storm roared in from the Gulf of Mexico with winds over 120 miles per hour, and a surge of water drowned over six-thousand people and destroyed many millions of dollars' worth of property. There were ferocious waves. Survivors, many of whom had lost entire families, were unable to bury their dead in the sodden ground. After several unsuccessful attempts were made to dispose of them, corpses finally had to be burned in great piles on the beach.

Our grandfather, Oliver Howard Bassett, was seventeen (17) at that time. He and his brothers had to help dispose of the bodies. The men would not be fed if they did not work. They built rafts to hold the dead, but even though they pushed them out to sea, they came back to shore. Thankfully, no one in our Bassett family perished. When the water came in their home, they chopped holes in the floors to allow the sea to anchor them down. They lost all their furniture. They stayed to help rebuild the City. The city built a seawall (7) miles and seventeen (17) feet high but as the town was only eight (8) feet above sea level, the sea wall had to be raised. In 1904, the tremendous project was begun.

In 1911, the year between the births of Bernice (1/9/0) and Helen Bassett (1/9/2), Hotel Galvez was opened. A wide causeway to the mainland was completed for tourist traffic, and an interurban train began operating between Galveston Island and Houston. The area where our Bassett family lived around Avenue M remains virtually as it was in the Nineteenth Century. Our German relatives arrived in Galveston (the Tusnors, Schulte's, Knoblochs, etc.) and settled in Texas.

In 1838, Galveston's harbor was considered the best in Texas. Galveston was an active port with ships of all sizes, and nation crowded its harbor. Cotton from interior plantations was stacked high on piers waiting to be shipped North and to England. Steamships were loaded with passengers going to and from New Orleans. Other ships were packed with immigrants (mostly Germans - Galveston was a port of Entry into the United States). The Strand became the most powerful business street in Texas and in the South. The wealthy people gave teas, dinners and receptions in their fine homes.

In 1860, census indicates there were about 2,000 slaves on the Island. Almost every white household owned at least one slave at that time.

In 1519 - Discovery of Galveston Island by Juan de Grijelva

In 1817 - Jean Lafitte establishes pirate villages

In 1802-1822 - Jane Long gives birth to first child of English descent while waiting in Bolivar Point for the return of her husband, Dr. James Long. That is why Jane Long is known as the Mother of our Country.

There is so much history in Galveston. We are proud that our family was part of that history and that they survived and we are here to tell about it. Your grandmother, May Agnes Merriman, and her family survived in the Bolivar Lighthouse. She was only fifteen (15) years old at that time.

At the time of the 1900 Storm - no warning was given to the residents of Galveston. The meteorologist had received a telegraphed message from Cuba and the storm. But he, "Isaac," paid little regard to it. Afterward, people called it "Isaac's Storm." So many lives could have been saved if he had only heeded that warning. Pop started working for the Southern Pacific Railroad in 1903. He and mom married August 17, 1905.

When the Great Storm of 1915 hit Galveston, Mom and the children were on the last interurbantrain going to Houston. Pop was going to come on the next one but he was delayed. Thank God. Because the next one that left sank. Mom had no way to know that he was not on that train until sometime later. No wonder Mom was always scared during bad weather. They moved to Beaumont, Tx. when Pop received his transfer in 1918. But even in Beaumont, parents and their children remembered if the weather got bad during the night, it would have them up and dressed. Bless all their precious little hearts.

We thank God for sparing our family during the 1900 storm and the 1915 storm. We are so proud of their courage before, during and after the storms.

Every family had different experiences. We hope we are all better prepared because of our family's experience. We know they had great faith and they loved us all so very much. Let's always make them proud. Stay Close - and remember - because they survived, we are HERE.

Thy word is a lamp onto my feet and a light unto my path.

Memories from George Lind

"I was born in Galveston but raised in Bolivar. I've been up in the lighthouse many times.

The final advance to the top was a ladder, and we were afraid to climb to the very top. We climbed up there, but the ladder was rusty and fragile.

We spent at least one hurricane in one house there. I always hoped someone would go up in there when a storm was coming as it would be so beautiful to see that water coming into the jetties. That would be something to see.

North of the lighthouse was a slough of water. We'd play baseball there as it was dry most of the time. Because of subsidence, there's water there now 365 days a year.

We also played on the Soldier Walk associated with Fort Travis and across that slough that headed to Bolivar and the grocery store. Only have to walk about 30 feet in some water.

Mr. Boyt had two children, daughter Sonja and son Patty, and they'd come down on the weekends with their horses, spend some time there, and we'd barbecue. Mr. Boyt was friendly. There used to be a monument in front of the light house and had something to do with Jane Long.

Somebody told us that Jane Long shot canons from there to frighten people away to make them think there were more people than was actually there.

Mr. A.C. Stanley, who lived not too far from the Catholic Church in Bolivar, he and a law enforcement person, a deputy or constable, went up in the lighthouse, round and round to the top, to apprehend a man who was wanted for a felony.

When we were kids, my dad told us not to look at the light because the murderer could reach down and get us. We believed it.

There used to be railroad tracks in front of the lighthouse going toward Winnie, but I never saw a train. My dad said he'd seen the trains heading north.

The residence closest to the ferry had a runaround built around it that was 20 feet off the ground. It was made of cast iron with pilings, and it didn't shake.

Oleander trees were planted there, and my brother and I cut the grass on the property."

- George Lind, age 77

> "I always hoped someone would go up in there when a storm was coming as it would be so beautiful to see that water coming into the jetties. That would be something to see."

"A passenger train stalled in the rising waters near the lighthouse, but only nine chose to enter the lighthouse, along with many residents of the Port Bolivar township.

The township was comprised of many in the fishing and shrimping industry that fled to the lighthouse for safety in storms. Ninety remained on the train and perished when the surge washed the train away."

- Russell Autrey

Memories from Randall Harrington

"I remember we had about 35-40 head of cattle in the pasture there when I was a boy. There was a slough or a pond there, and we'd catch mud oysters out of Horseshoe Lake and sometimes redfish.

The lighthouse has been an icon for Bolivar as far back as I can remember. My dad was overbid by the Boyts and Maxwells. He was disappointed when we didn't get it because we were going to live in one of the houses. It sold for considerably more, but I don't know the amount. In the 1950s, a group in Galveston purchased Fort Travis and later operated a motel using the old barracks. I did yard work for them for a while around the motel. Fort Travis was later acquired by Galveston County and later made into a park. The old ferry landing on South West corner was used as a fishing pier. The motel didn't last long, and the pier was badly damaged by a storm and never repaired.

There were two houses there, one was for the keeper and one was for the assistant keeper. They were up on high pilings so they wouldn't be affected by the tides. Those houses have been there as long as I can remember.

The Maxwells used one of the houses as a summer house, and the Boyts had the other one. We used to go in the lighthouse back then. There was a circular stairwell that went to the very top with quite a few steps that were not for the faint of heart. It was a lot of fun and a real thrill to get up that high and see the water.

The old Fort Travis was still there until the government took ownership back. That was in the 1950s. My grandmother was born in Galveston in 1893 but lived in Fort Bolivar all her life.

The lighthouse is quite an icon for Bolivar. People stop and take pictures on Highway 87. That's a sight of Bolivar you normally don't see."

- Randall Harrington, age 83

> "The lighthouse is quite an icon for Bolivar. People stop and take pictures on Highway 87. That's a sight of Boliver you normally don't see."

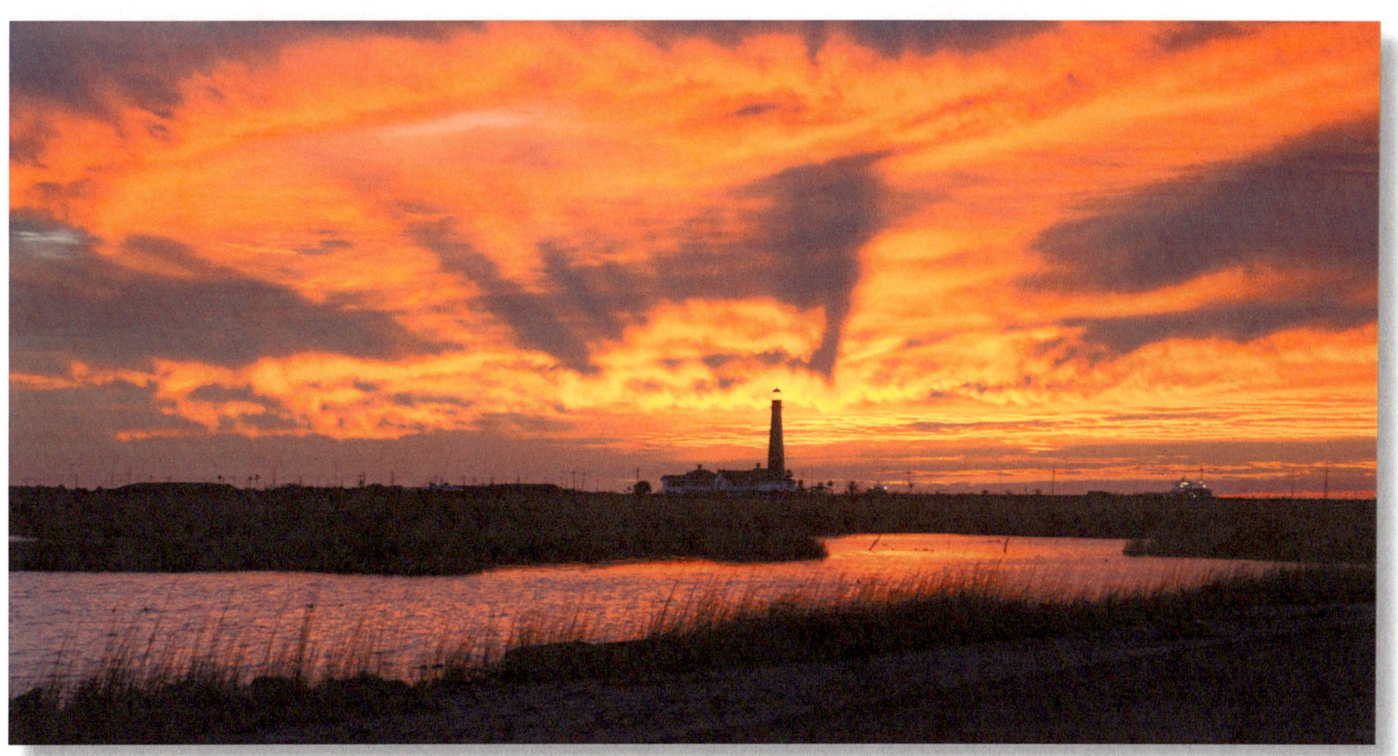

Memories from Sylvia Comeaux

"I think every kid has broken into the lighthouse at some time. One Halloween, somebody hung a dummy over the side and people thought something bad had happened.

I remember picking crabs out there in the water with my sister. I do remember looking in and seeing the rusty stairs. There were cisterns out there, and I was terrified I'd drown in one of them.

There were so many kids back when I was growing up out there, at least 10-12. This was their playground.

> "The lighthouse is ours. We all love the lighthouse or maybe we belong to the lighthouse. You see it every day. You wake up and see it, get out of the house, and it's there."
>
> - Sylvia Comeaux

The company decided they didn't need the lighthouse anymore and it was of no use.

The story is that the bulb went out and it was replaced, but the replacement light wasn't as bright. That got replaced with a brighter bulb, and that's in the Smithsonian.

My dad's brother, George, worked for whoever was in charge of the light. He turned it on and off, and he was the one who turned the light off for the last time. That was so sad."

- Sylvia Comeaux

Memories from Robert W. Bouse

"When we were kids, we walked everywhere we went. There was a school up here; it was an old wooden school house. My granddaughter would've been the fifth generation to go to that school.

There weren't a lot of houses out here back when I was growing up. Grandpa had an old store, a two-story building. He was the postmaster and had a grocery store. He came in 1909. It didn't make any difference who came by, that's where they stayed. Had a porch all the way across the front, and the breeze blew like crazy. Must've had about 15 beds in there. After he gave it up, my Aunt Dixie Shaw ran it. The building is still there.

My father and his family lived in one of the lighthouse houses. He was a lighthouse tender. Back then it was kerosene, not electric, and they had to carry the kerosene up there in cans and fill the tanks that kept the light burning. The reflector was what made it so bright.

My father never complained about working there. He was an easy-going person. He liked to teach people how to do things, and he taught me lots of things. They had a baseball team, and my dad played on the team. They played Smith Point.

They'd play different places – Winnie and here.

There used to be lots of oysters down here. Shrimp and oysters were the main things we caught.

There was a windmill here and that was the way we got water for the cattle. When it got really dry, the water got bad, so they'd use a windmill to pump the water. It would be so cool coming out of the ground.

In all the years I've lived here, I never went up in the lighthouse. My mama told me if I went up there, I'd get a spanking. I heard Daddy had his initials carved up there, RCB Junior. I'd like to see that one day.

They say whenever that light came around back then, it lit up all of Bolivar, that's how bright it was.

My wife, Jerri, grew up in Mississippi. She's been here since the late 1970s. This house we live in was built in 1901. We paid $12,000 for this house. We love seeing the lighthouse every day.

Before I die, I'd like to go up in there."

- Robert Bouse, age 84

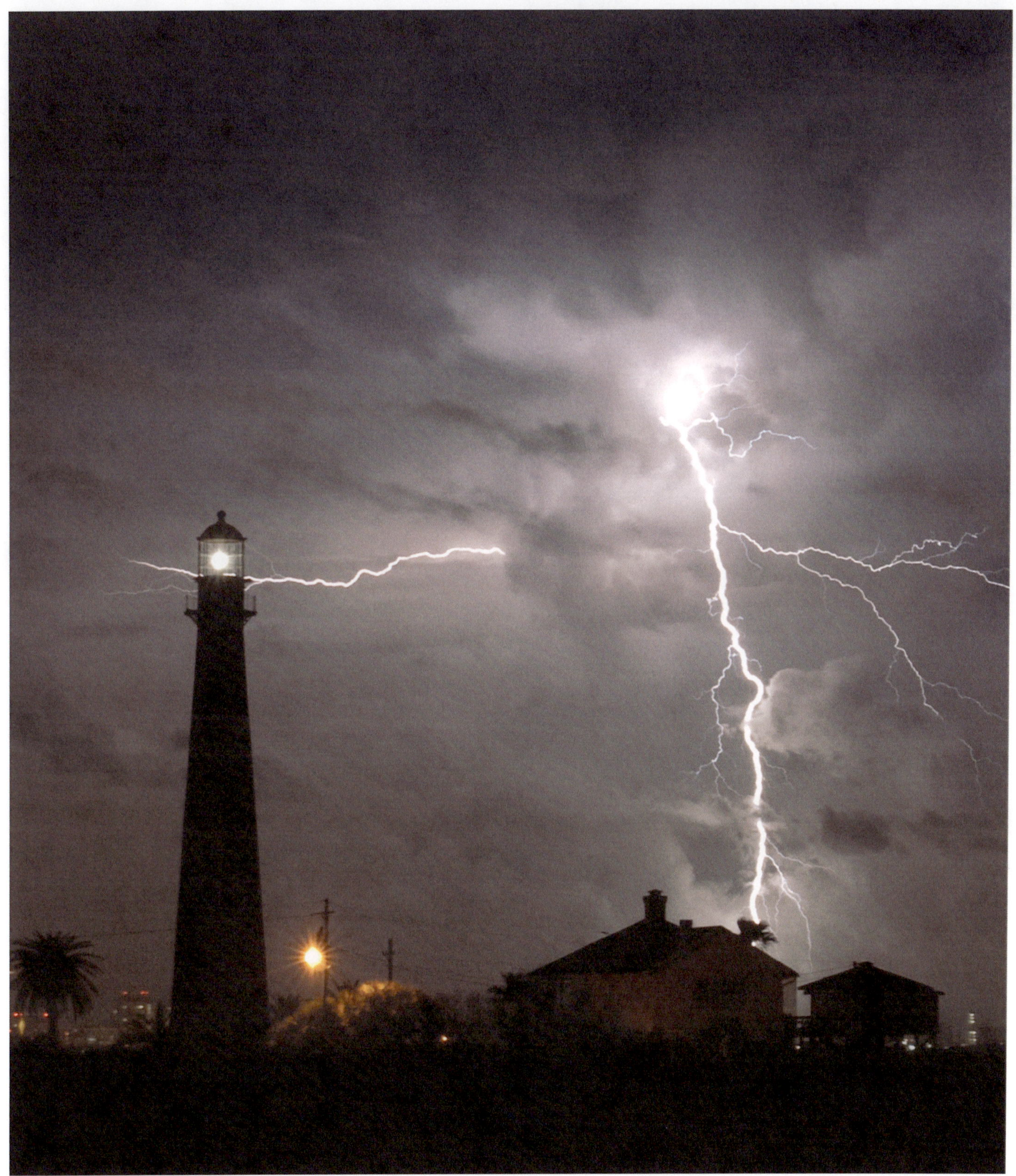

Lighting storms are spectacular on the peninsula. One of the roads on the peninsula is Frenchtown Road. The name came about when a cannery opened half a mile down the road. Many French and Cajun workers moved to Port Bolivar from Louisiana to work the shrimping and fishing boats as well as the cannery. Because there were so many French-speaking people now living on the peninsula, the name was a natural choice.

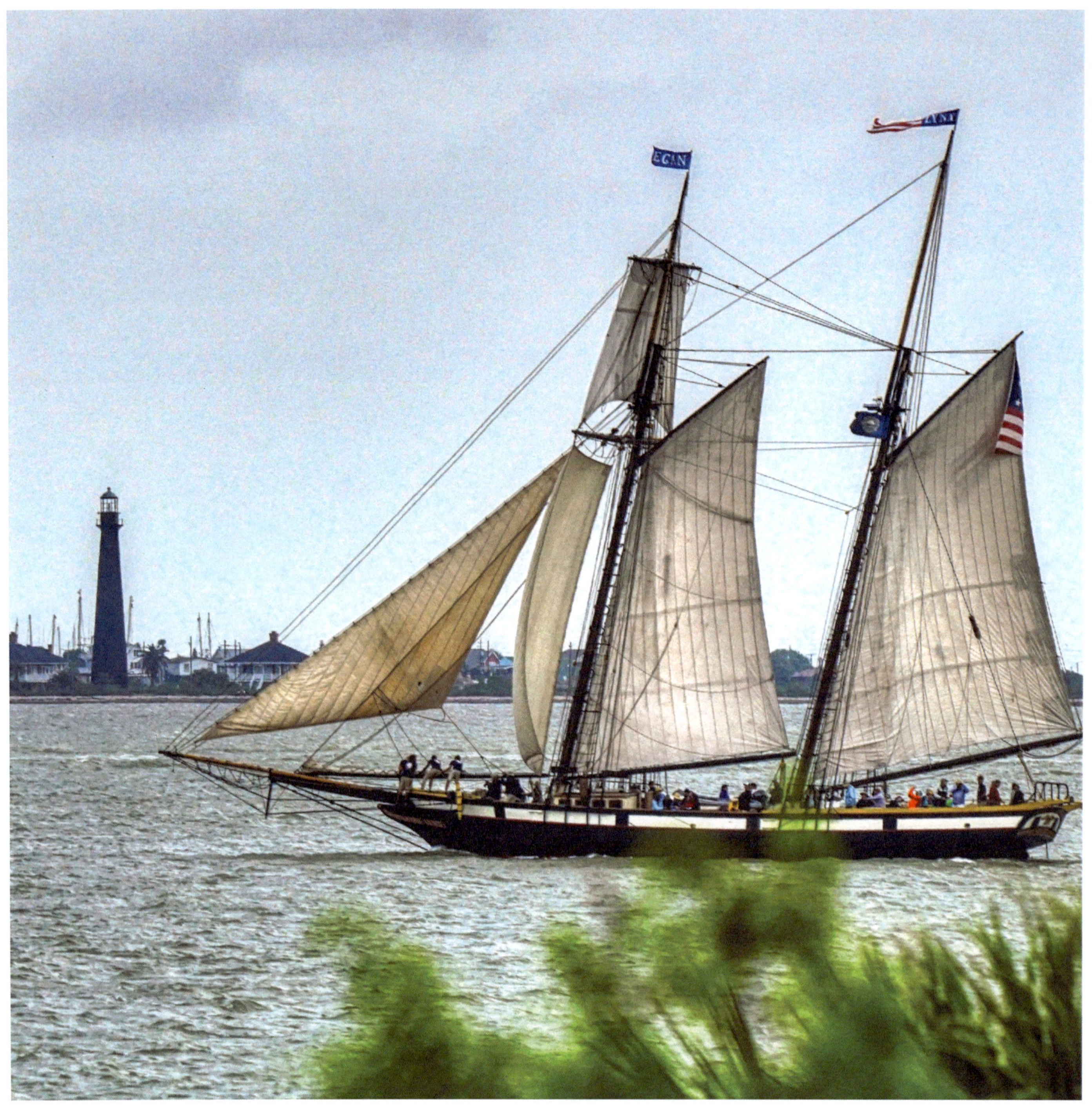

Sailing Ships of Old

From sailing ships to floating oil derricks, the lighthouse has seen untold thousands and thousands of ships passing through the narrow channel between Bolivar Point and Galveston Island. The far point across at the channel was once called "Fort Point" after French pirates built a dirt fort there.

Iron, Steel, and Wood

A towering steel off-shore oil derrick floats past the old iron-clad tower of light while on the facing page a wooden ship glides by with the wind as ships of old did in decades past.

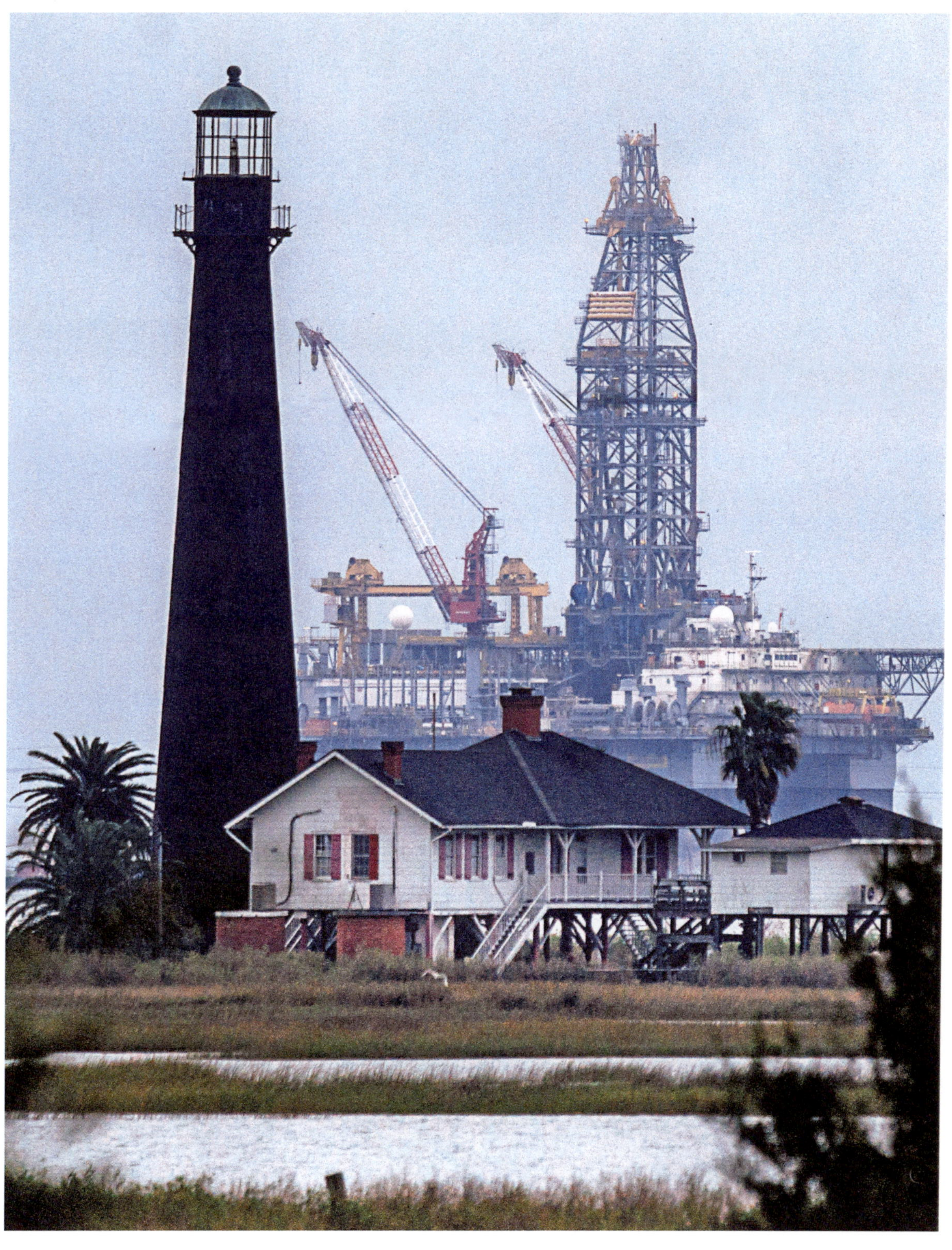

Riding out the 1900 Storm

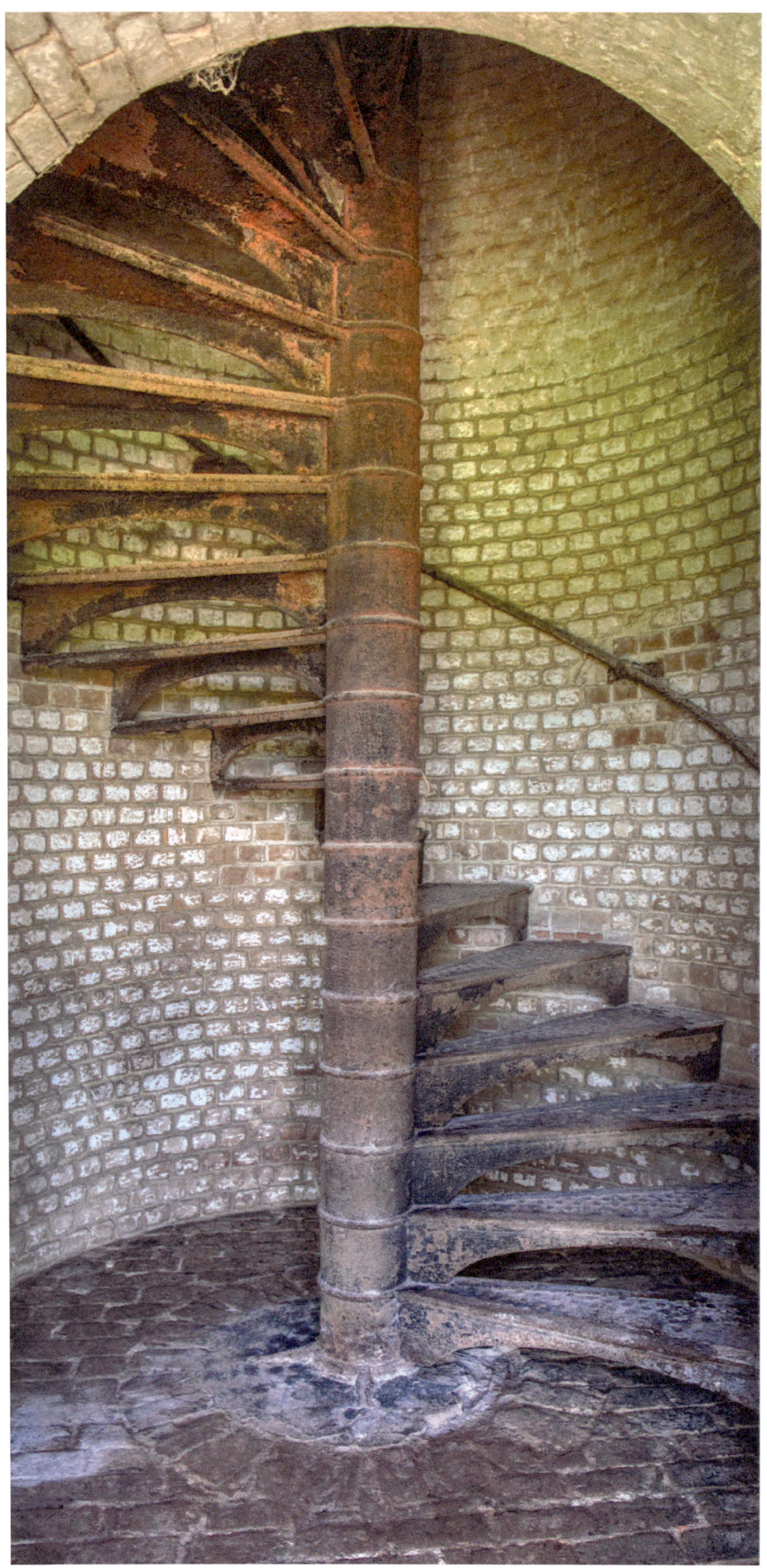

"When you look inside the door of the lighthouse, you will see the circular stairwell centered inside the lighthouse. These metal stairs were home to 125 people during the 1900 storm who sat two per stair.

If the wave height was anything like Hurricane Ike in 2008, the people riding the storm out would have had to climb to the 15th stair and be just out of the water. With the wind, which must have been howling inside and out of the lighthouse, the waves hitting the lighthouse, rain coming in through the windows from above, it had to have been miserable for all of those hours until the storm passed but they at least survived.

It has been mentioned that during the storm, the iron door on the front had been forced open by waves or debris which, if left opened, could have caused damage to the brick masonry creating a catastrophic failure of the lighthouse interior. Someone entered the flooded water and was able to resecure the door saving the interior and storm dwellers.

Once the storm passed, the keepers' dwellings, the food and water provisions, and probably any mode of transportation, was gone. The survivors then had to survive the aftermath of the storm and wait for help to arrive. The stories that came afterward are just as bad as surviving the storm. It was enough for people to pack up and move away from the coast for good."

- Pete Chase

Memories from Lloyd Maxwell

My grandpa, Elmer Boyt, had lots of the property down in Bolivar. The government was selling off war bonds after World War II. The brothers, Elmer and Pat, made a bid on the lighthouse and beach houses. They got the lighthouse, two houses and two acres for $5,500. That was a lot of money after World War II.

We used to go down to Bolivar in the early 40's. Grandpa Boyt had a two-story ranch house about 6 miles to the east near where the Bolivar Yacht Basin is located, and we'd stay there. Mom and Dad would take us to the beach one or two times during the summer. There wasn't much at the end of the island. The beach houses had been abandoned in the mid-1930s because the lighthouse had been decommissioned in 1933.

The first time I remember of any consequence was when mother and daddy took us to see the lighthouse we'd purchased. That was in 1946. I was 7 years old. The place was in shambles. There was a piece of fence around the property, and everything was grown up. There were two old out-buildings there which used to be the privy, and the houses looked like an owl roost because they looked terrible. The windows were knocked out, doors were off the hinges and a lot of the slate shingles on top of the beach house were broken. People had gone up in the lighthouse and knocked the windows out. They'd taken bricks out of the inside of the lighthouse and threw them at the beach house roofs too.

But the old lighthouse impressed the heck out of us. The lighthouse still had some of the white paint on it. It was originally painted black and white. I remember when we got down there, we said "Momma, what are we down here for?" She said, "We bought this place. We like the lighthouse but we're gonna fix it up."

The inside of the houses have exactly the same lumber that was in there originally. There's no artificial timbers inside the house; it's as it was built back in 1915. The ceilings are 13-feet tall, and the house has triple floors and double walls and they were well built. All the wood inside the house and around the porches is original wood.

When we got the beach houses, Mother and Uncle Pat used Grandpa Boyt's carpenter crews to repair them. He had a big ranch and crews in Liberty County. He ranched cattle in different counties. In the winters, he used his crews for repairs, and they got the beach houses back together. This was in the winter of 1946 to the early spring of 1947. It started looking pretty dadgum attractive. They got the beach houses finished in the spring of 1947. The houses were painted red with some white trim. They rehung the doors and they were just about ready for us to move things in when Texas City blew up.

There was no electricity down there, not until about 1953-54 when Gulf States built a line from High Island to the lighthouse area. We'd go down every couple of weeks until harvest time and spend a couple of days there on the beach. We had to take our drinking water in glass water jugs. When they fixed up the beach houses, they put indoor plumbing in. We had cisterns and gutters so we could use rainwater to wash our hands and dishes and to operate the bathrooms. We had to use Coleman oil lamps at night. We had screens on the windows and ceiling fans. It was hot in the daytime, but there was a good breeze at night. The beach houses were nice, and we enjoyed the devil out of them.

I'd definitely like to see the lighthouse restored. It's going to be 150 years old in 2022. There's a lot of history there. So many people would drive down there and talk to us about their grandparents who survived in the 1900 and 1915 storms. If they hadn't survived in the lighthouse, they wouldn't be here.

We have always enjoyed being at the lighthouse. My daughter, Ann, was in Seattle a few years ago and she saw 3-4 different pictures of our lighthouse and the beach houses in a gift shop there. She told the clerk that her family owned the lighthouse and one of these beach houses. The woman was so amazed. The lighthouse is known all around the world.

- Lloyd Maxwell, age 82

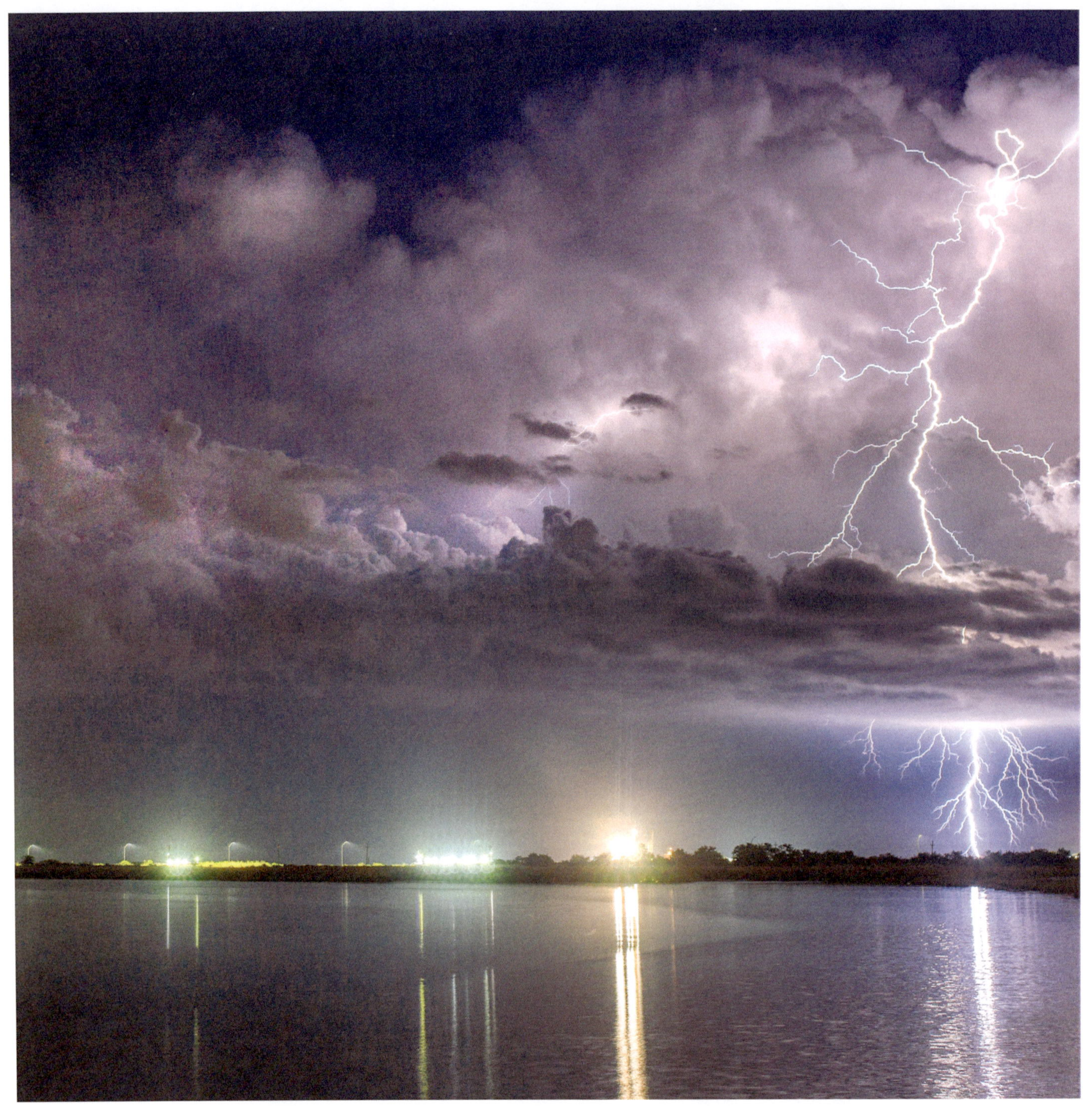

Memories from Mark Kelso

This is family "scuttlebutt," but my great-grandfather's oldest brother, James C. Kelso, was the county road and bridge superintendent during the time of the 1900 storm. We think he took people off the train that came down to the peninsula.

As the water started rising, family folklore says that he took people off the train in Bolivar and took them to the lighthouse to ride out the storm. They all survived. His brother, Munson, and two of his nephews did die in the storm. My great-grandfather was James's youngest brother. There was 18 years between them.

When my dad was a kid, he used to ride his bicycle over there. He and his friends would take the ferry and go to the lighthouse and sneak in.

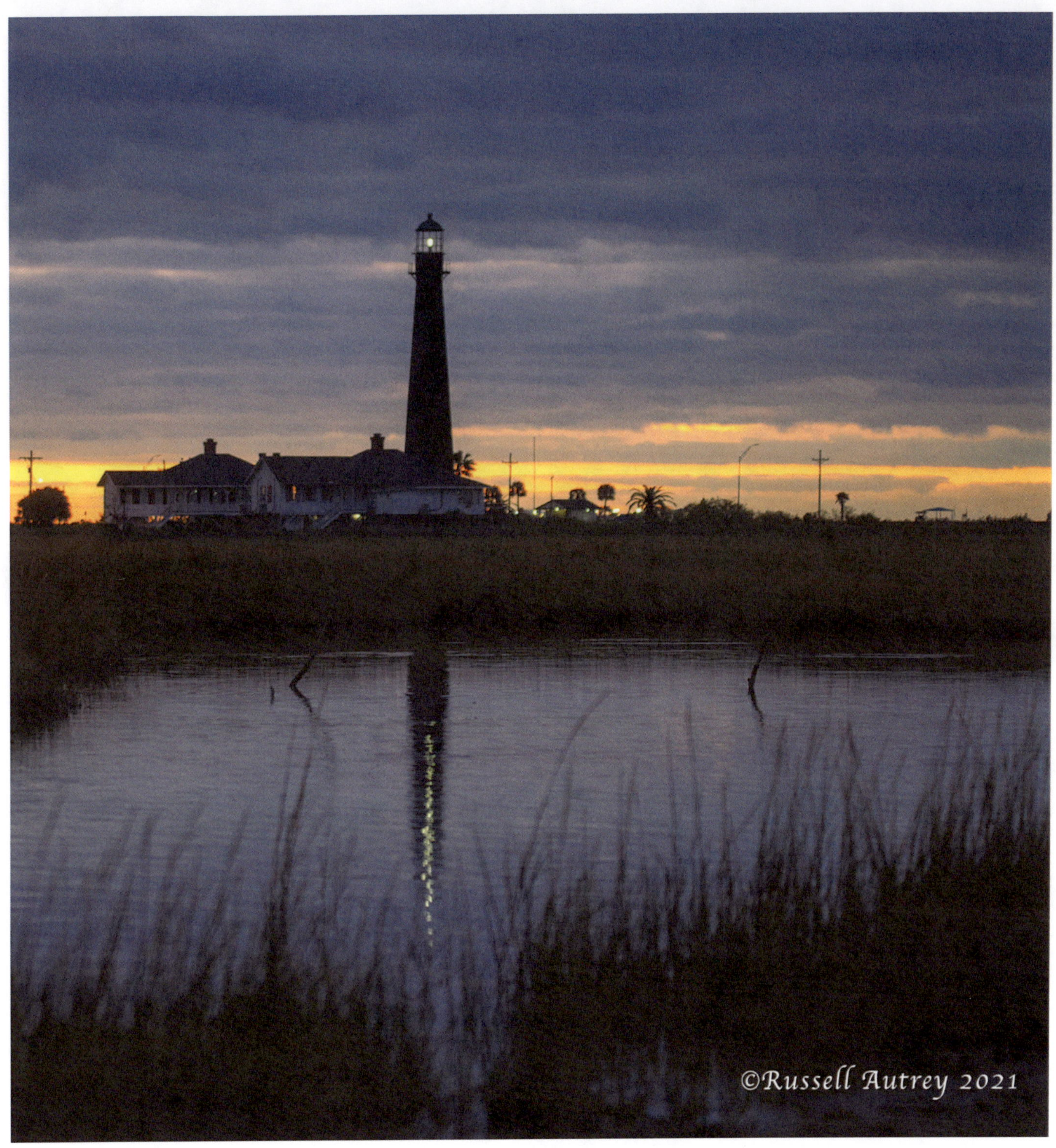

The Bolivar Point Lighthouse is deceivingly large. Most vantage points make it seem like it's only about 60 feet tall but it's actually about 10 stories tall. When you walk up to it and stand at the base then look up towards the top, you finally get a feel for how big it is. It had to be a massive feat to build it back in 1872. The brick masonry inside is fascinating to see. Try to picture the masons laying the brick all the way up towards the top back in those days or the guys bolting the huge metal plates together with wrenches then welding the seams with whatever process they used back in 1872. I always ask how in the world did they get those pieces up to the top back then. With the third order Fresnel lens shining out across the peninsula, it must have been amazing to see!

      - Pete Chase

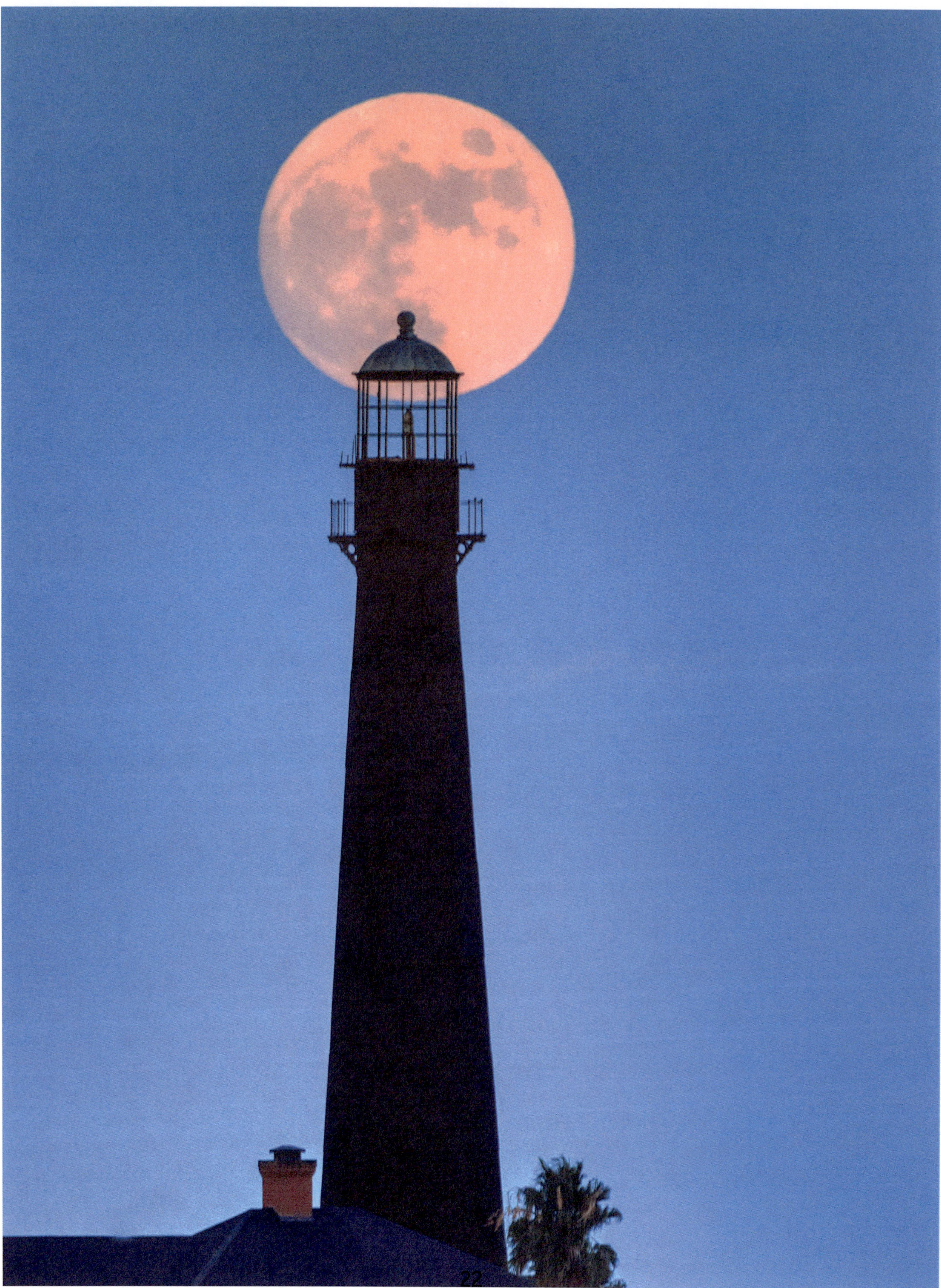

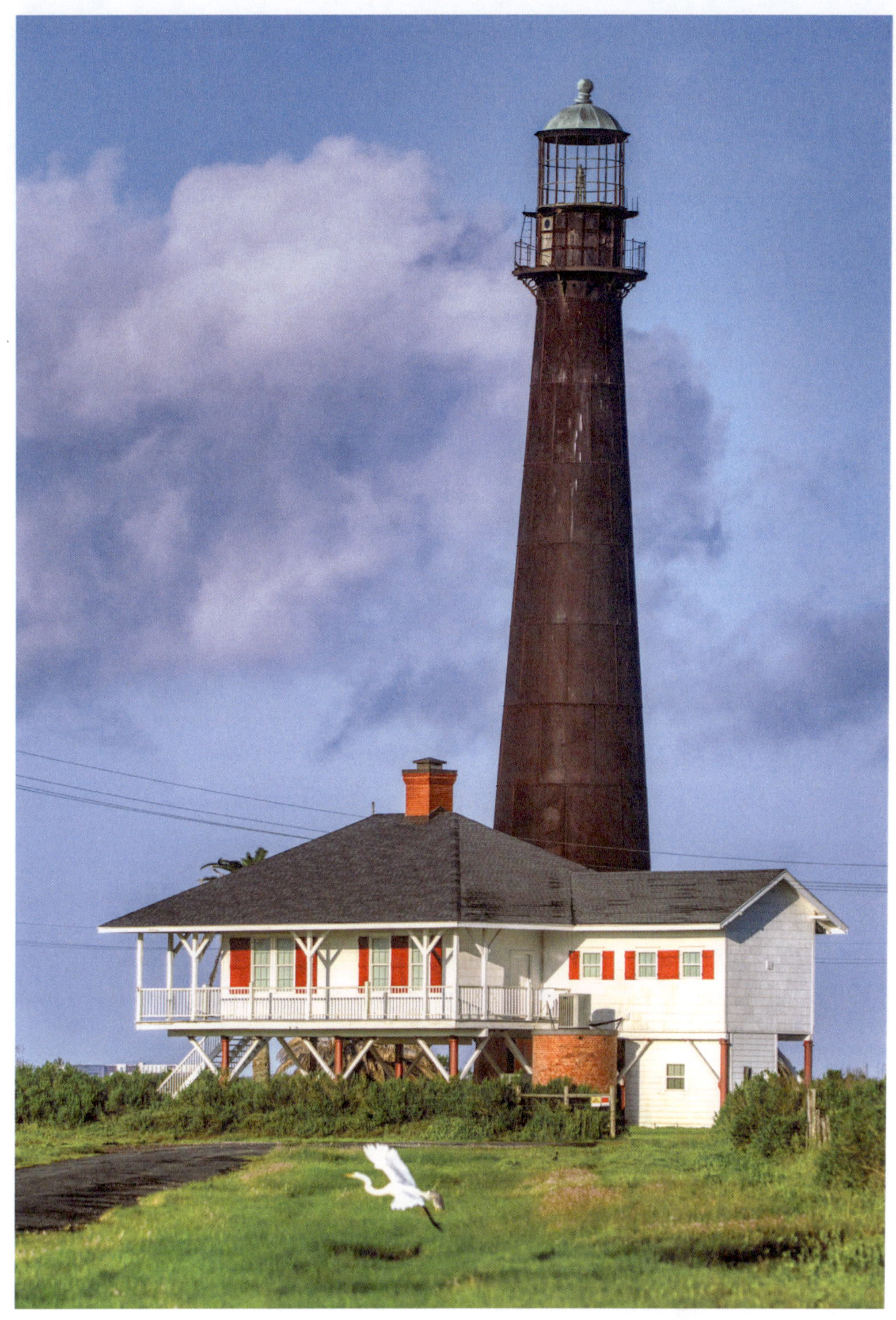

"The first lighthouse on Bolivar was built in 1842 and dismantled by Confederate forces during the Civil War. With none of the original pieces ever discovered, it was probably melted down for war efforts. In 1872, the tower you still see today was built. It served until 1933, and the Lighthouse properties sold as government surplus to Elmer Boyt in 1947. Today, the keepers' homes are still privately owned by family members. The tower itself is under the helm of a 501(c)(3) foundation, the Bolivar Point Lighthouse Foundation." - Russell Autrey

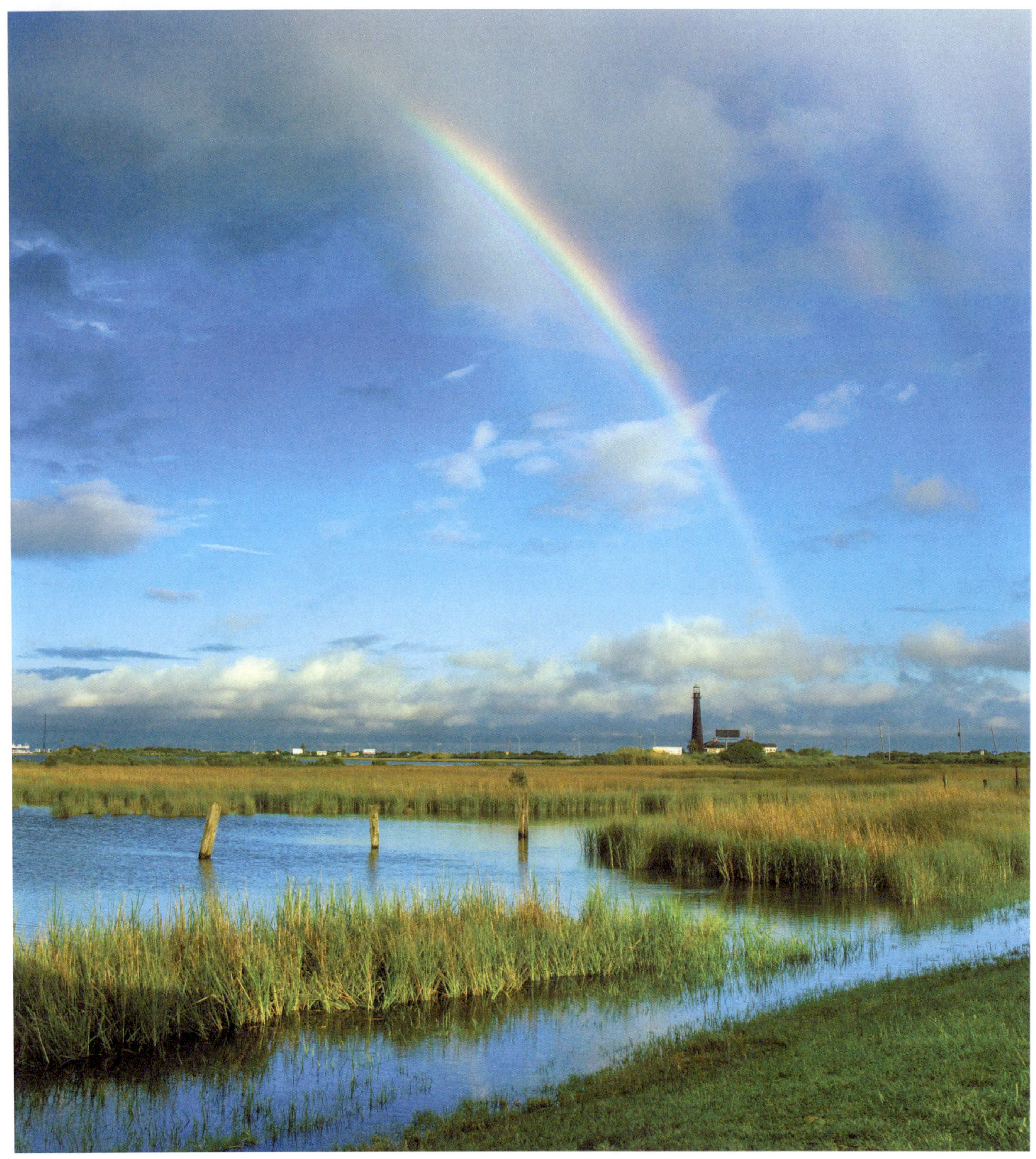

"Standing at the back sea wall of Fort Travis, one can see East Galveston Bay on the left. The area is known as Bolivar Roads as barges and ships cross in the shipping channel. Galveston is out of sight on the far left, and the Gulf of Mexico is a few hundred yards behind. A ferry is loading at the Bolivar ferry landing as a rainbow lights the sky above the lighthouse. The shallow slough in front is a popular fishing area for many of Bolivar's shore birds and also a few crab-eating raccoons."   - Russell Autrey

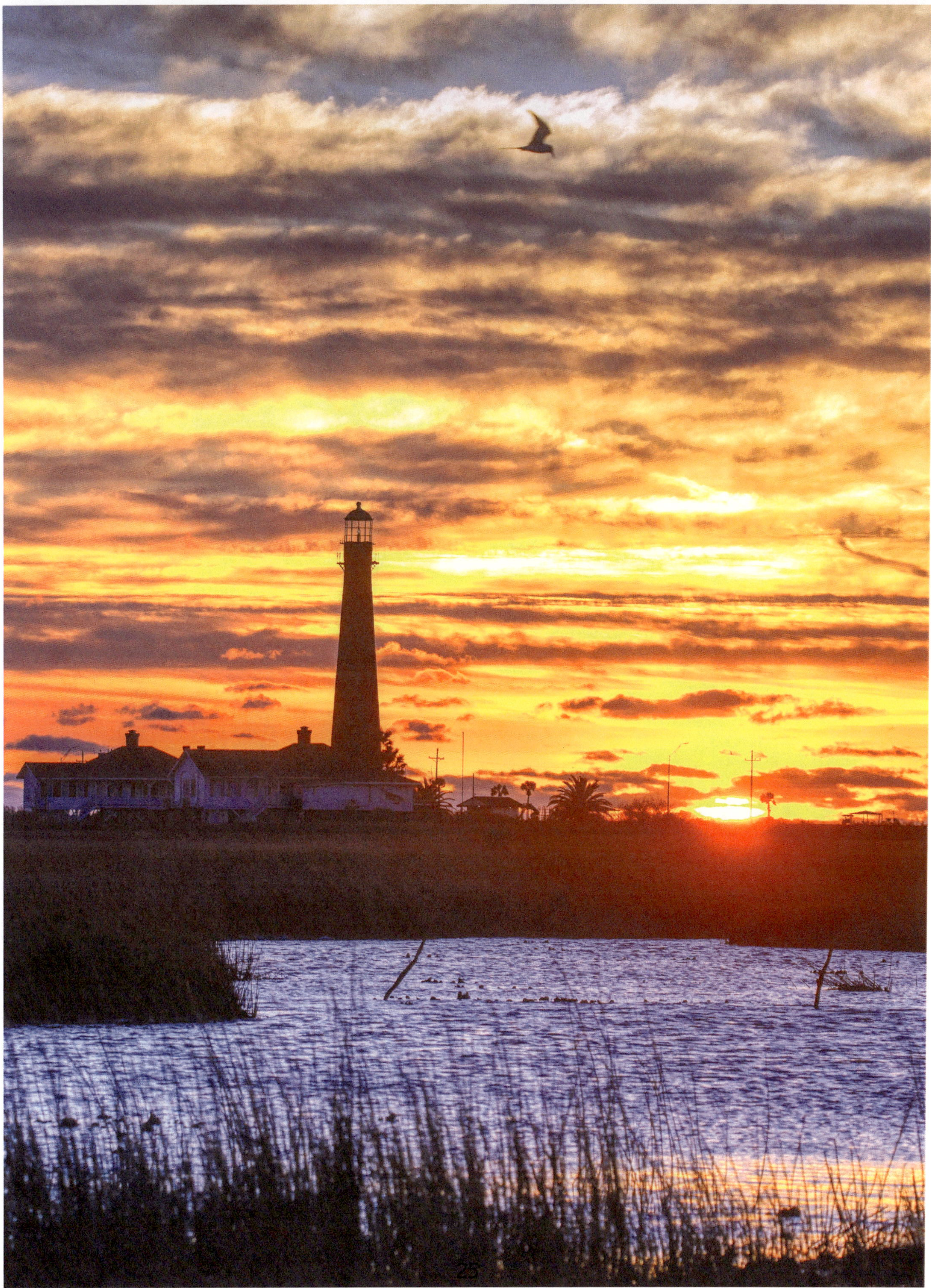

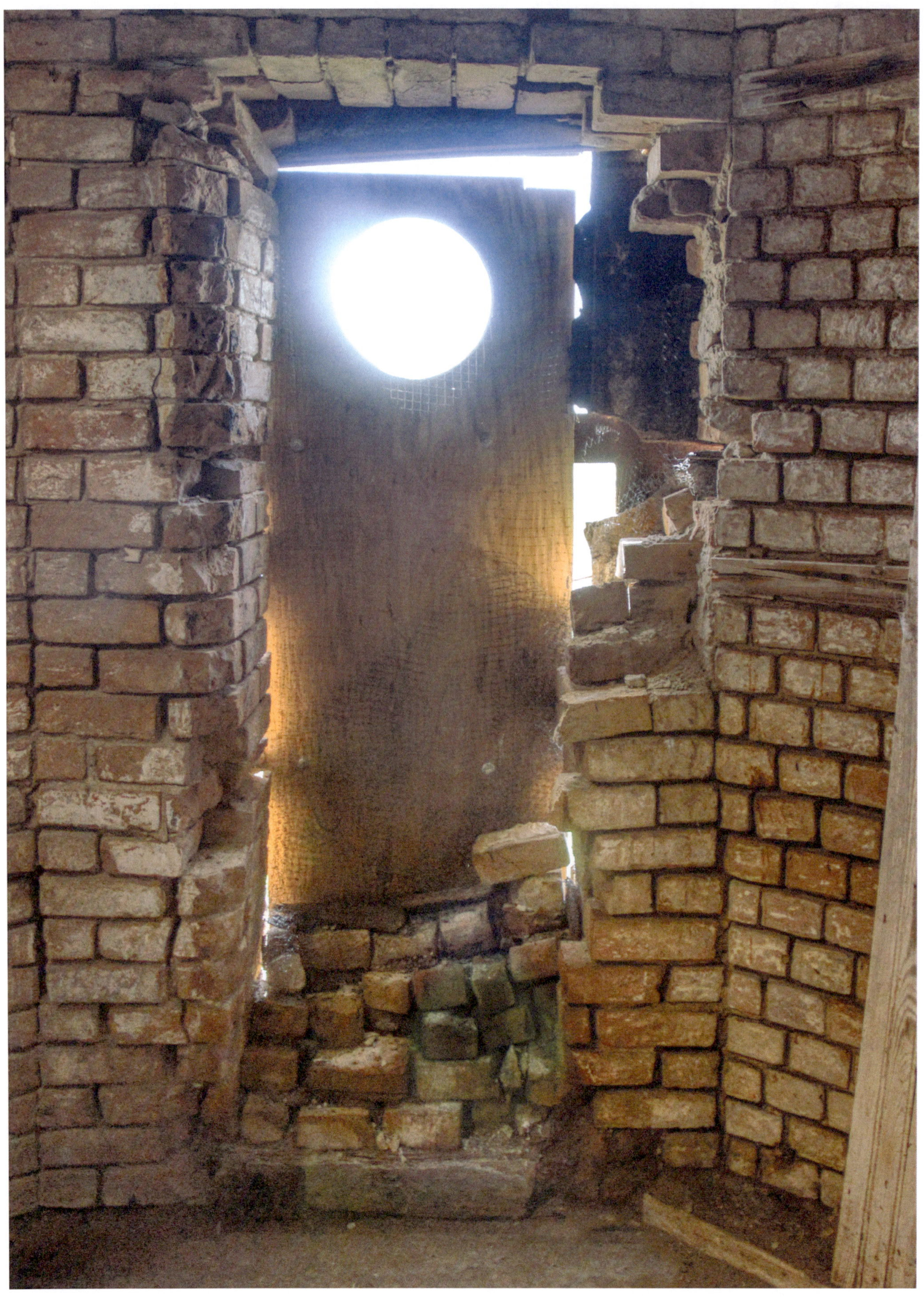

Memories from Mark Boyt

"The lighthouse holds a special place for me. We spent big chunks of our summertime there as kids, five to six weeks, until it was time for the rice harvest.

Originally, it was painted black and white. The first level on the inside is still white. In the old photos, you can see a windmill and a cistern. The windmill cistern was for well water that we used for our cold water in the house. Additional cisterns on the houses collected rain water that we used for hot water.

They'd collect water there. There used to be two rows of bricks around the base of the lighthouse, but they're all gone now. Souvenir seekers or tourists, we think.

At one time, there was a curtain around the light during the day. They were worried about a fire from the reflection.

In 1917, while the houses were under construction, the Army accidentally shelled the property from East Galveston. One shell landed in the yard and one hit the lighthouse. Fortunately, they were only practice shells. You can see the patch on the inside if you know where to look.

The Coast Guard was still running the navigation signal until it was decommissioned. In 1933, the Coast Guard moved out and the U.S. Army took it over.

I asked my grandmother once what she thought of the house. She cried because all the glass was gone. It was the year of the Texas City blast. It had just happened (1947). The tip of Bolivar is not that far from Texas City.

In 1947, our grandfather bought the lighthouse from the government, and George Maxwell got the other half. The Boyts and the Maxwells are joint owners.

I feel responsible for the lighthouse. My brother and I owned half of the lighthouse, and we've been going down there our whole lives. It's like a second home.

The lighthouse has always been there.

> "Time has a way of undermining all the works of man. It's incumbent upon us as the overseers to do something about it. If we don't, it'll all be gone."
> - Mark Boyt

It's such a durable monument. Time has a way of undermining all the works of man. It's incumbent upon us, as the overseers, to do something about it. If we don't, it'll all be gone.

My cousin Amy volunteered to manage the process. We all have full-time jobs and it takes a full-time job to get things going. The Bolivar Point Lighthouse Foundation was established to preserve and restore the lighthouse. There were no grants or track record. Initially, there were donations from family, but now we're getting more.

We have an architectural plan, and we have to make it safe. Doing that means we'll have to take the top two levels off and rebuild. We'll leave it to the professionals to make it look like it was. That'll be tough on the community.

We're going to get some attention, and we can't do it without the community's support. We need lots of help. It's all about the lighthouse and creating a visitor experience where people can come and go up in the lighthouse.

I invite people to check out the virtual 3D scan on the Bolivar Point Lighthouse Facebook page." People love lighthouses all over the world. After the Alamo, this is one of the most photographed sites in Texas.

It's a part of the peninsula that's the most visible. It's distinctive, and we are the families that own it. We understand what it means to people. We want to save and restore the lighthouse and make it better. I've never seen it with glass in the lantern room. If we did nothing, the top would fall off but the lighthouse would stand." - Mark Boyt

** The Bolivar Point Lighthouse Facebook page was established, and is maintained, by Mark Boyt with over 3,000 followers. The Bolivar Point Lighthouse Foundation was established in 2015 as a 501(c)(3) non-profit for the purpose of preserving and restoring the lighthouse. The foundation's web site is www.bolivarpointlighthouse.org.*

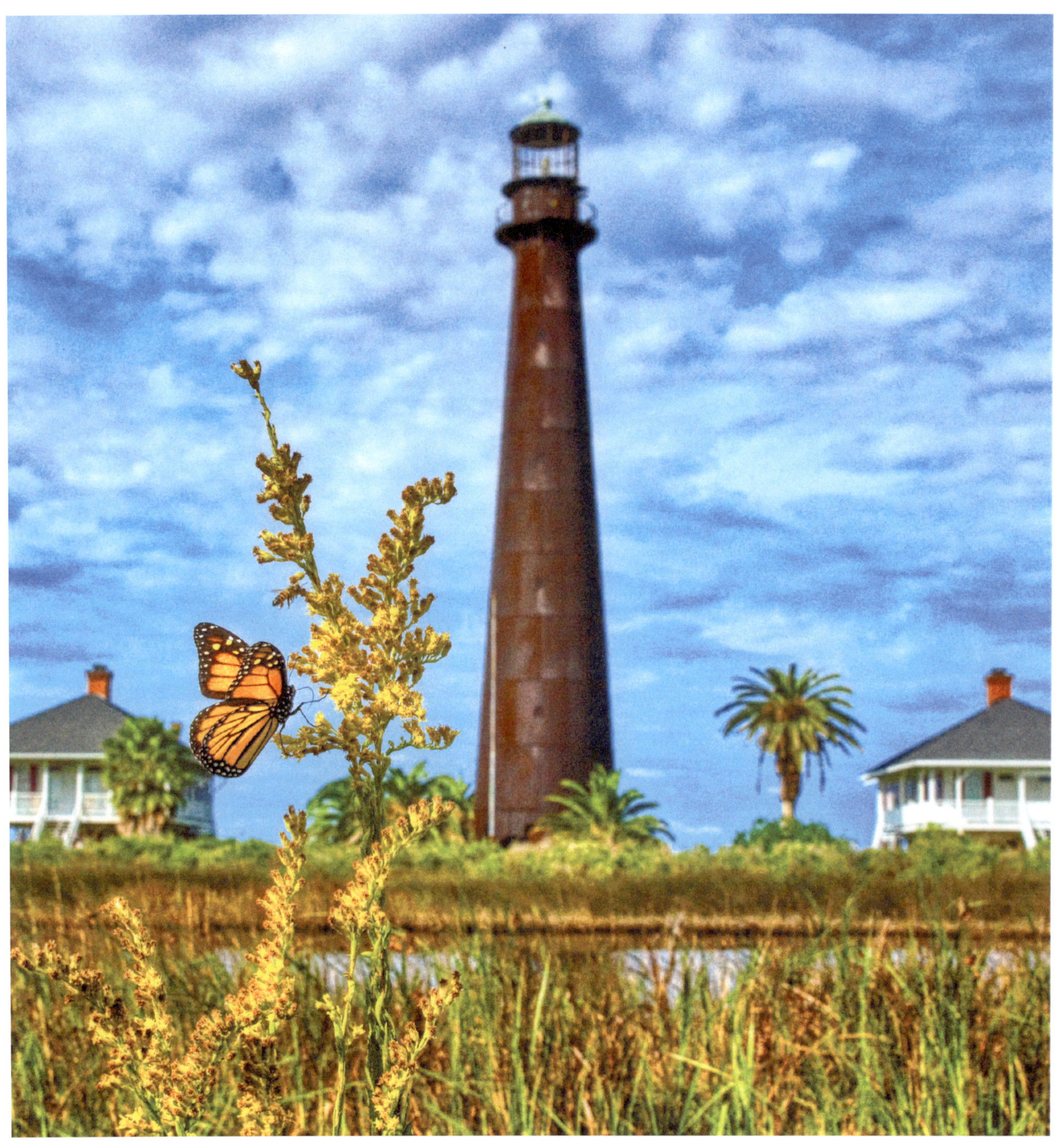

Many people don't realize this almost 150-year-old lighthouse is actually the second lighthouse on the property. The first was also iron clad and about half the size of the current one but was dismantled to salvage the iron for the Civil War effort and to keep the Union Army from controlling Galveston Bay.

After the Civil War ended, the current lighthouse was erected in 1872 to guide ships and commerce to the thriving Port of Galveston. The Port of Houston wasn't built until after the 1900 storm. After the 1900 storm, they decided to create a port with more protection from storms further inland toward Houston. - Russell Autrey

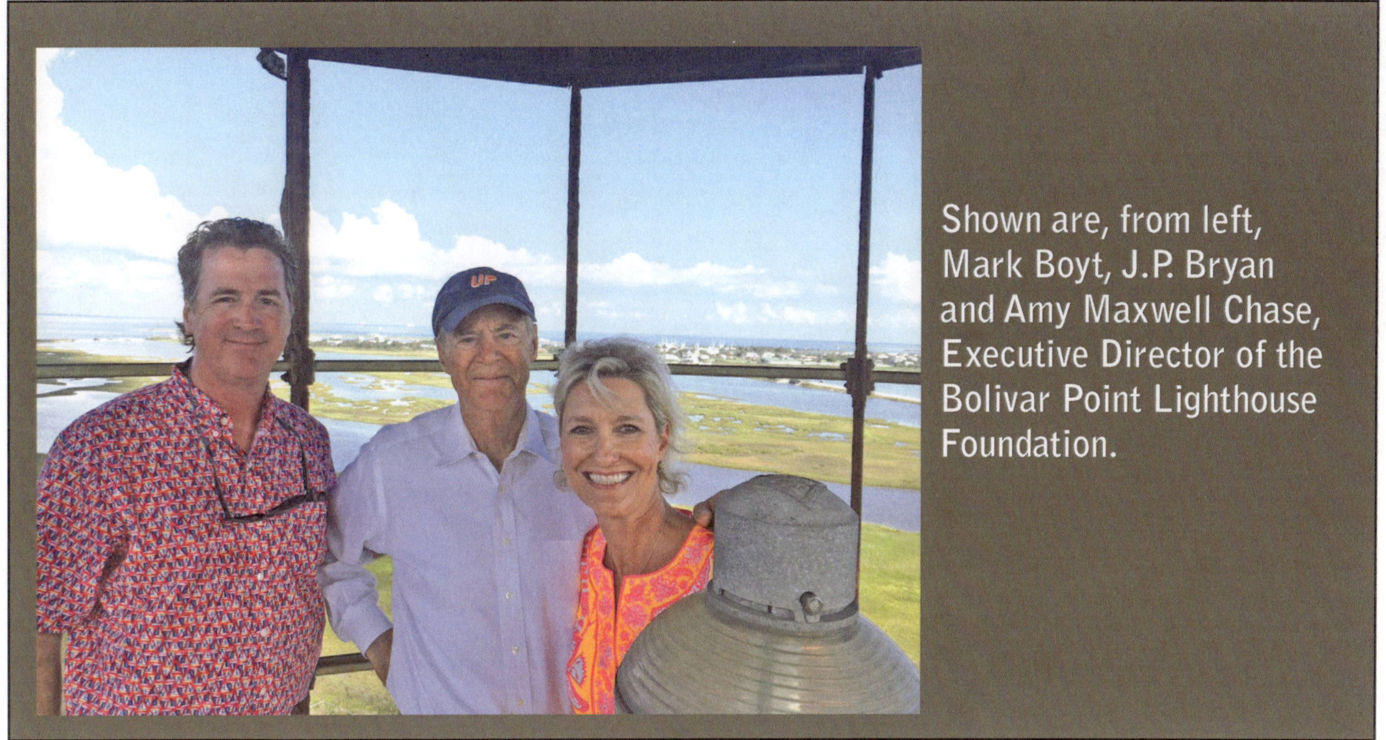

Amy Maxwell Chase, far right, is the great granddaughter of Elmer Woodard Boyt and the granddaughter of Ila Boyt Maxwell. She has had a lifelong relationship with the Bolivar Point Lighthouse. Amy graduated from Texas A&M University in 1996 with a B.S. in Marketing. Her primary duties as director of the foundation are coordinating and directing the restoration planning and execution, researching available funding, and directing the pursuit of funding that is in line with the foundation's mission.

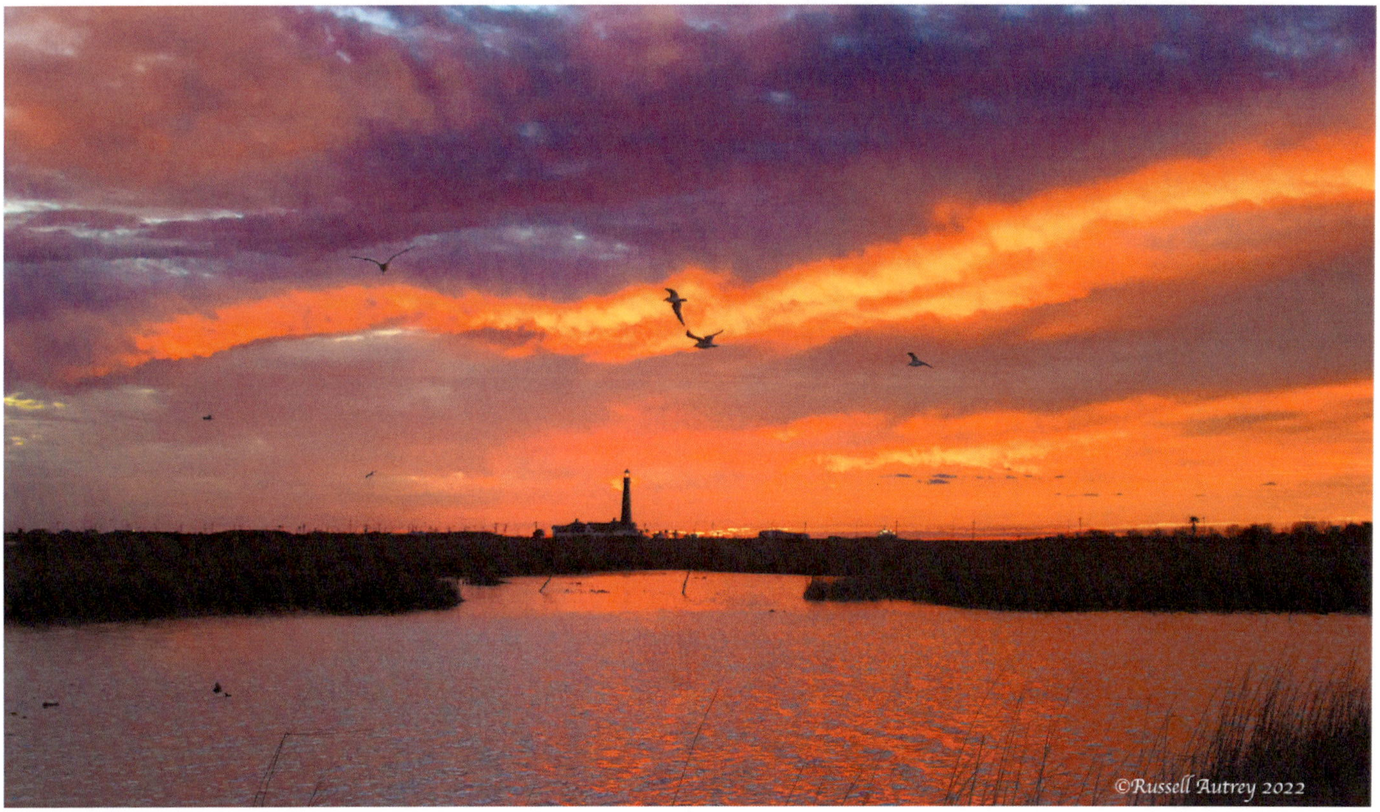

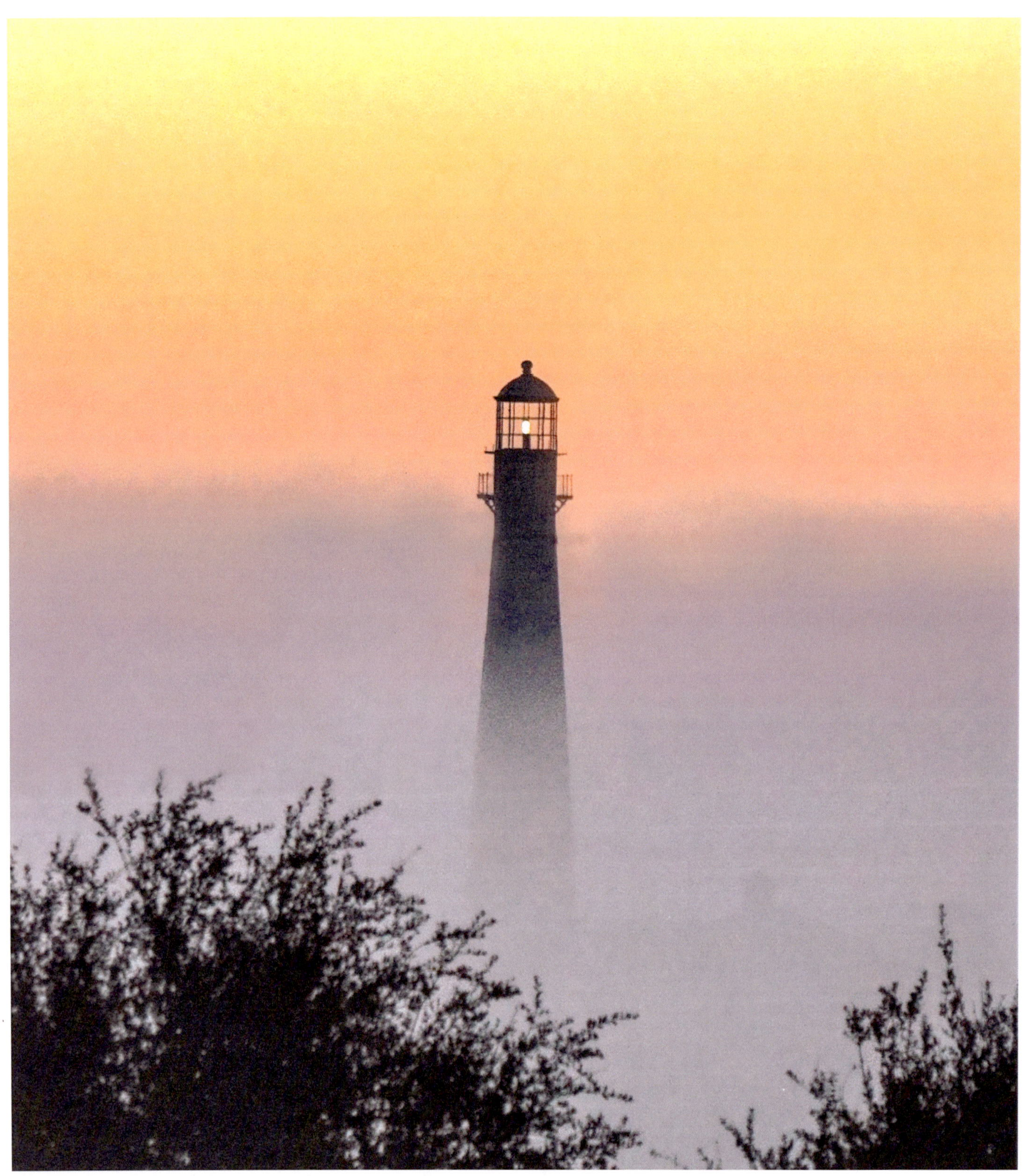

Eight beams of light passed through the Fresnel lens every 15 seconds when the lighthouse was in daily use. Fueled by kerosene, the intense light was from the burning gases in a mantle. In its 61 years of duty, the light only went out for two nights. During the 1915 storm, 11-foot tides burst through the door, and the kerosene tanks floated away in the raging waters, never to be found.

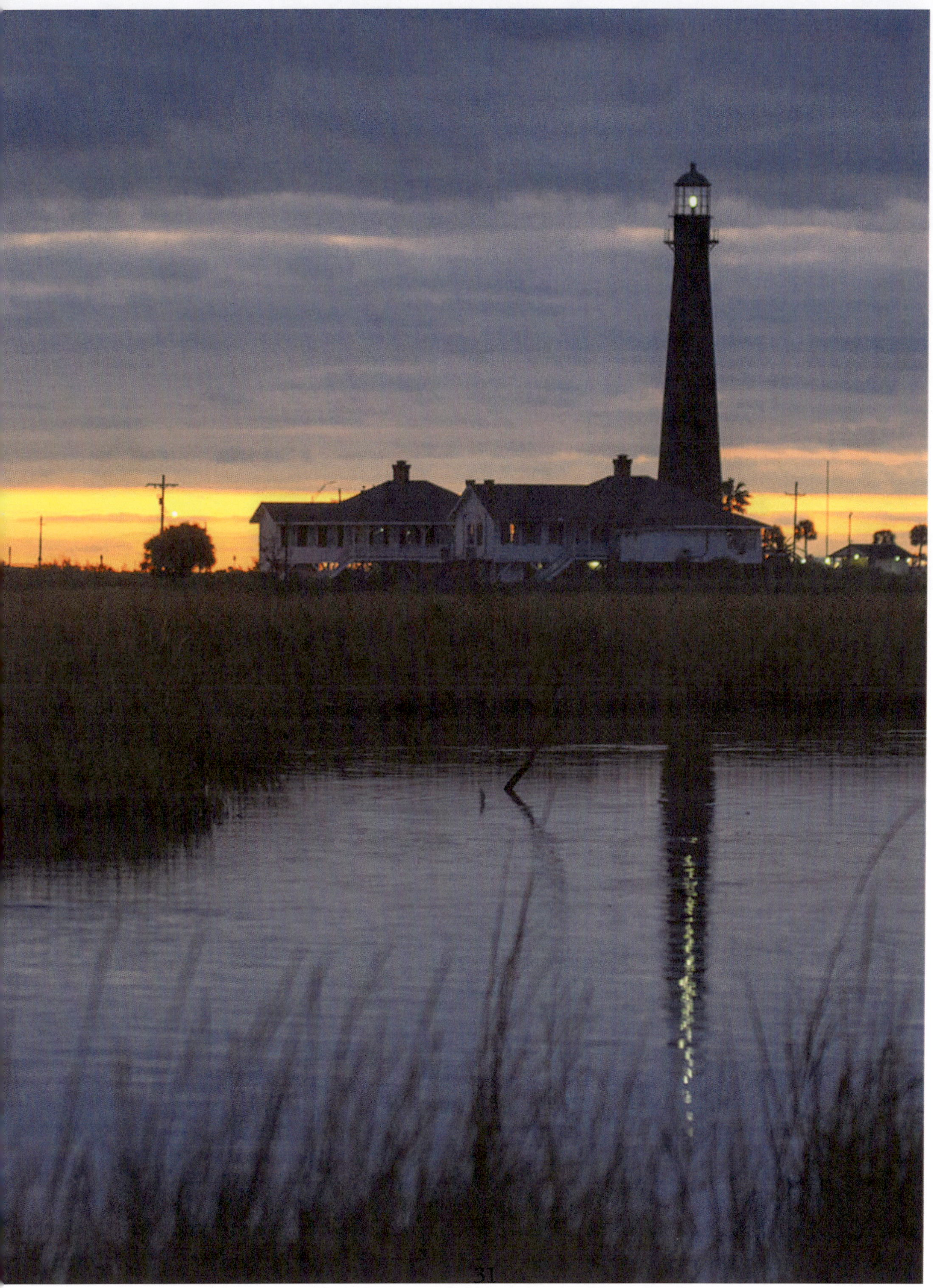

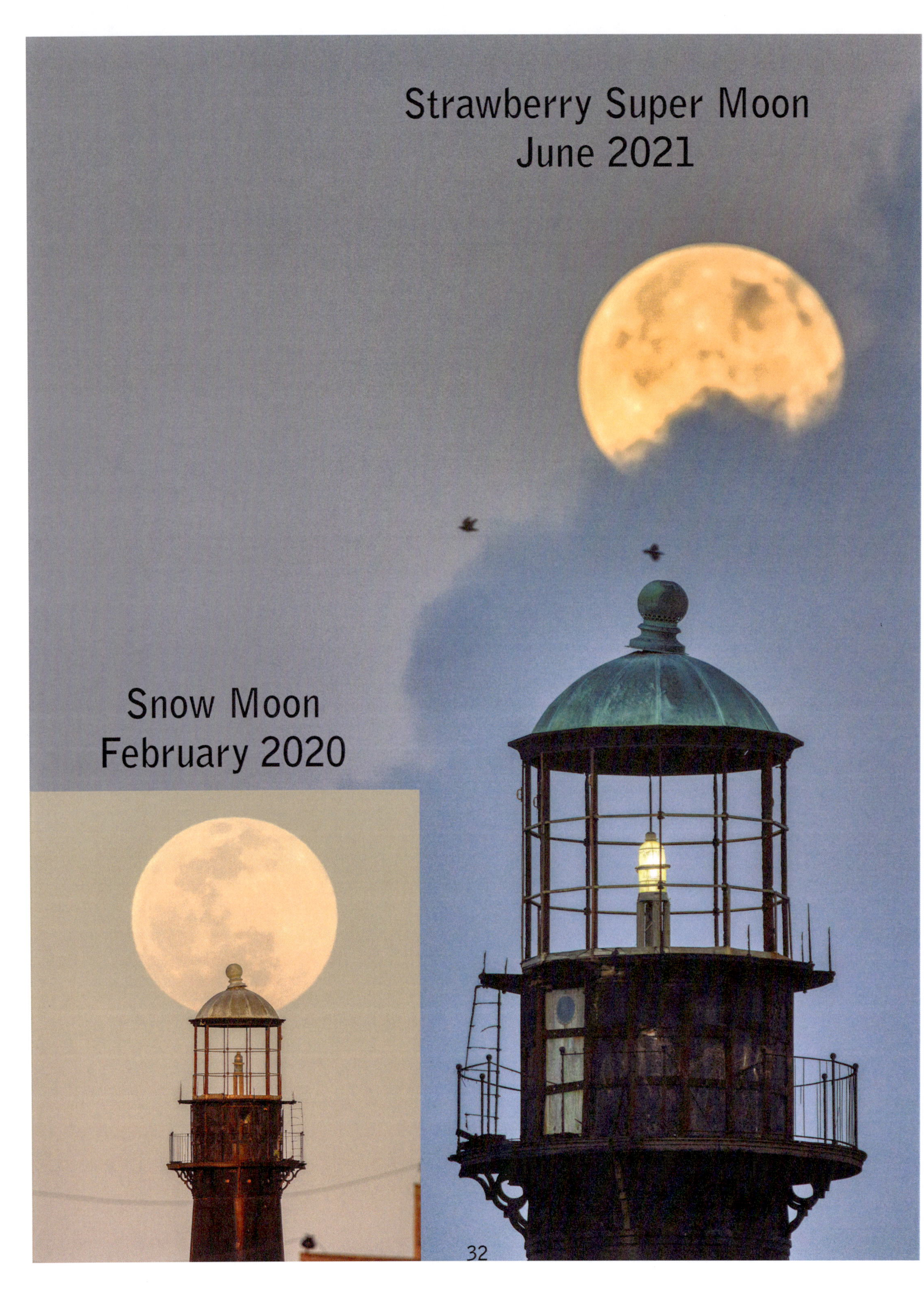

Strawberry Super Moon
June 2021
Snow Moon
February 2020
32

Hollywood Comes Calling

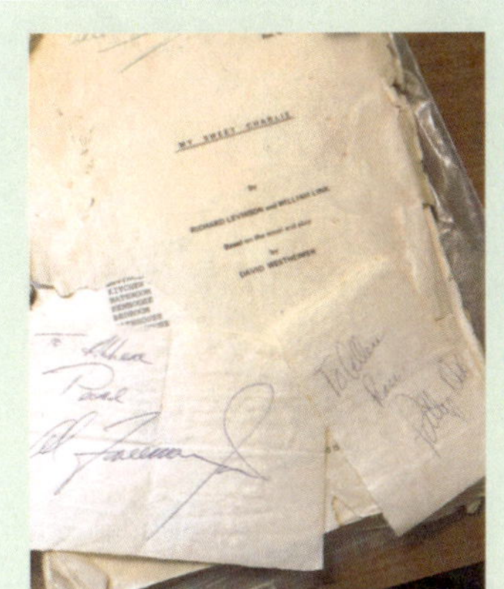

Alleen Williams has a signed script from "My Sweet Charlie" that was filmed on Bolivar Peninsula.

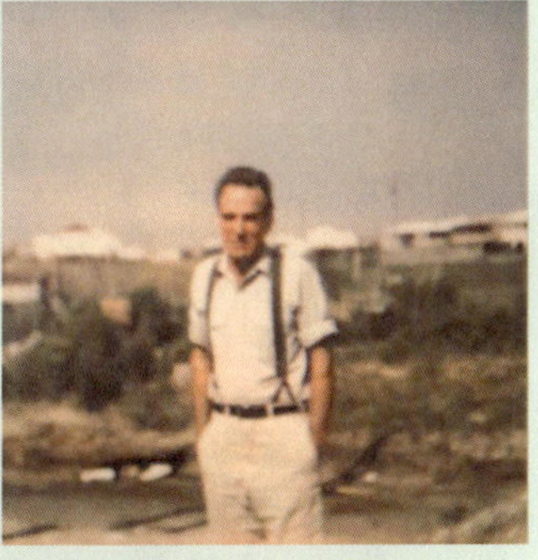

Ford Rainey also starred in "My Sweet Charlie."

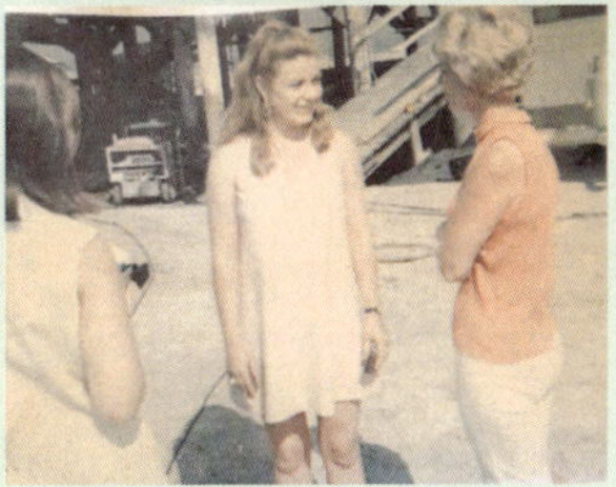

Alleen Williams, far right, chatted with movie star Patty Duke many times while she was on the peninsula filming. Duke won an Emmy for her performance in "Sweet Charilie" and Al Freeman Jr. earned an Emmy nomination.

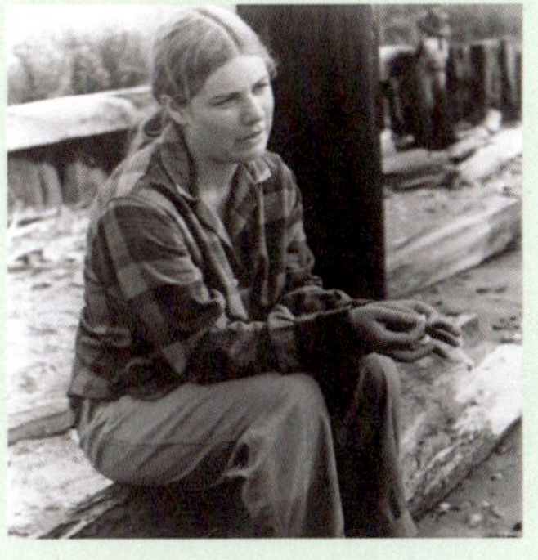

Patty Duke starred in the movie.

All photos courtesy of Alleen Williams.

"The movie was exciting for me. I had a friend whose parents owned a bait camp at the jetties, and they shot a lot of the movie down there. My friend, Cora, and I were there every day. Her parents owned a bait camp. For somebody from the country, it was exciting because I had three children. I was probably in my 20's.

"It was fascinating watching them make the movie. They'd have to do a take over and over again, and I thought 'how boring,' but I'm sure that's the way every movie gets made. I'd never been around anything like that before. I remember watching them and remember seeing Patty Duke walking down the road to the lighthouse.

"We got to meet all of the actors. They were really nice people. Patty Duke was just like anybody around here. She talked to everybody and never acted like an actress. One day, we were standing there, talking to her, and somebody wanted to know if I wanted a picture. I said I did and I still have that picture of Patty Duke and me.

"The weather was terrible. It was cold and windy. I remember Cora and I made a stew or gumbo and they all ate. Cora's mom, their last name was Roberts, had food for the crew there as well as at the bait camp. They sold soft drinks and chips for people who were fishing, so they (the film crew) were in and out of there every day.

"There was Van Lucen's down on the corner of the highway, and they were there quite a bit. He had gas and it was like a bait camp, and they filmed a little bit there.

"The biggest part of where they filmed was at the lighthouse and bait camp. There weren't that many people there, like tourists, in Bolivar at that time. Mostly, the people there were people who lived there. The movie people probably stayed in Galveston because there wasn't a place for them to stay in Bolivar.

"It was a lot of fun watching them make the movie. They were really nice people. They asked if I wanted a script, and I told them I did. They all signed it."

- Alleen Williams - age 81

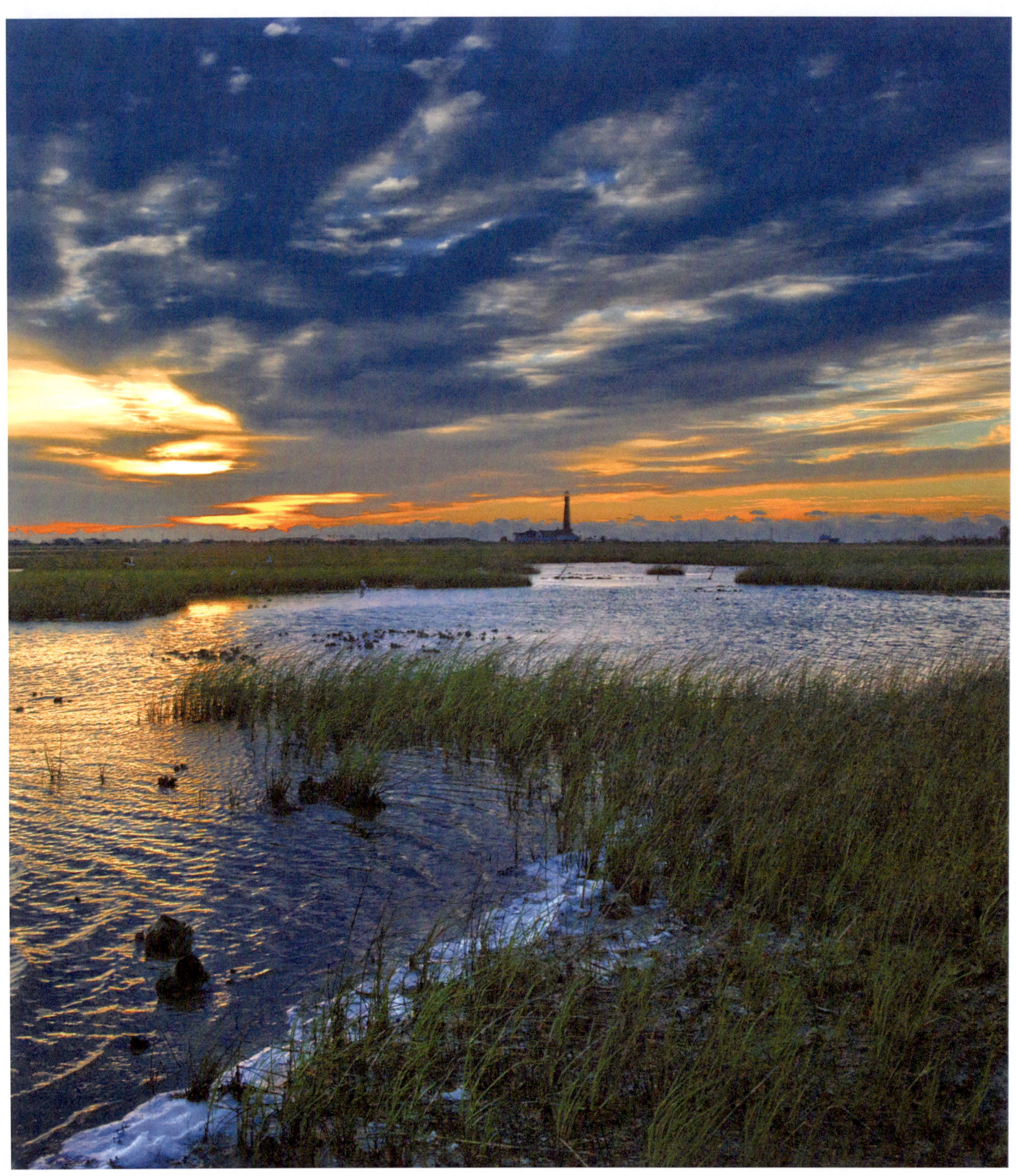

North of the lighthouse is Horseshoe Lake. Replenished by tidal flows from the bay, the marsh is home to a variety of shore birds that feed in Horseshoe Lake. Anglers enjoy fishing in the lake while kayakers and canoers enjoy the quiet waters to fish or simply paddle. The lake is filled with oyster beds and small crustaceans of all kinds including shrimp, crab and barnacles. Flowing in with the tides are mullet, drum, flounder, hardheads, and many varieties of salt water fish. The lake is open year round.
     - Russell Autrey

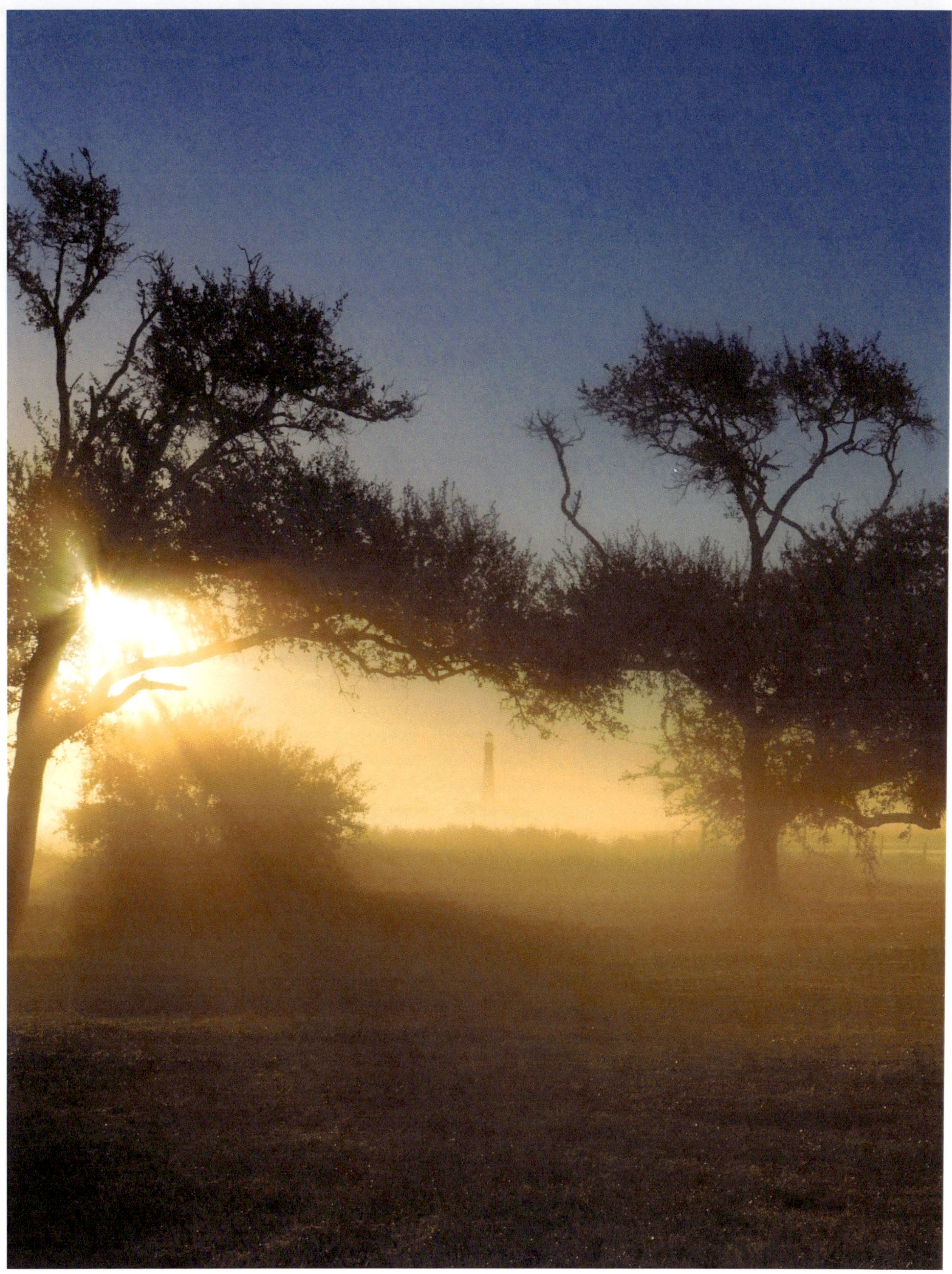

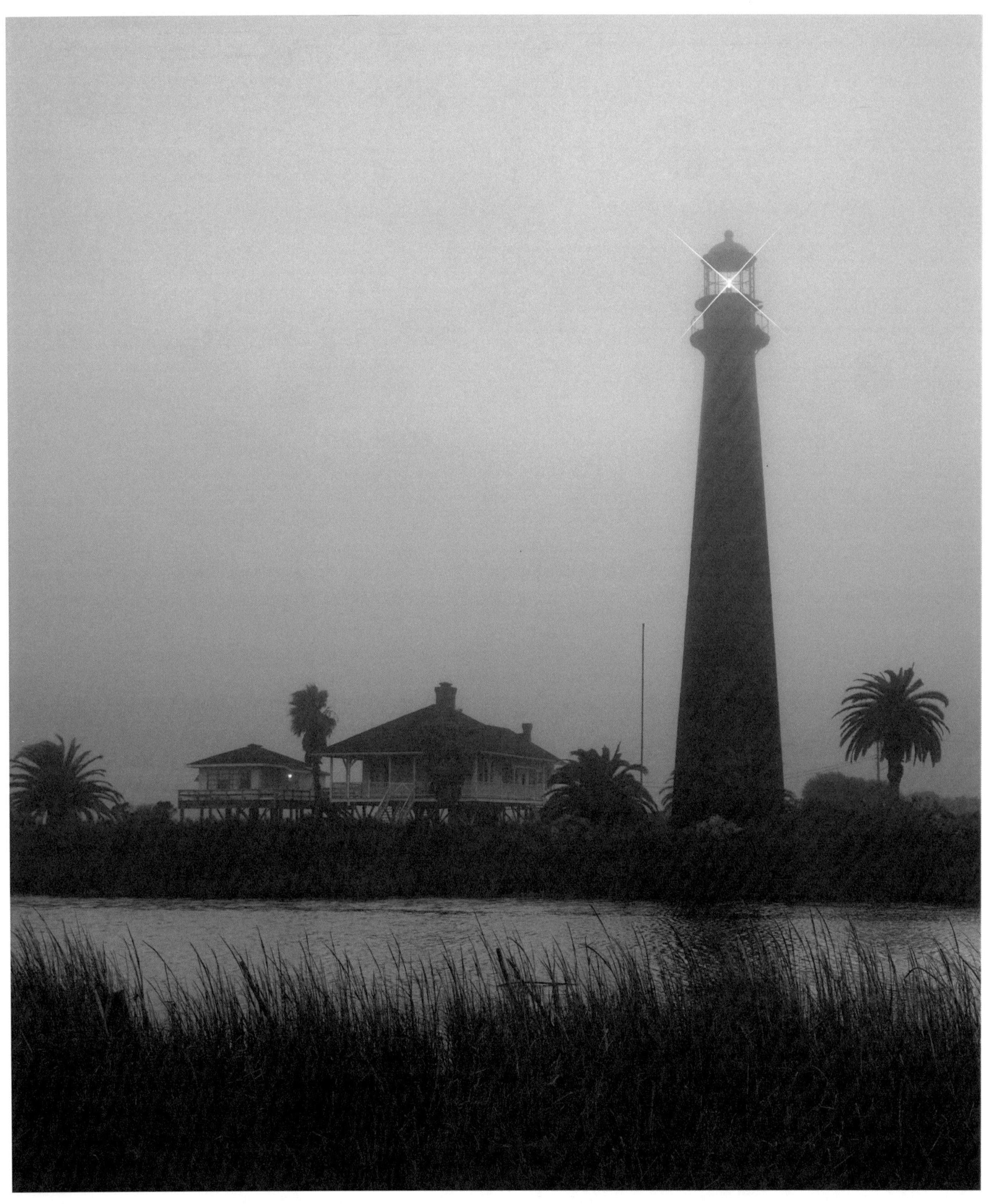

A light still shines from the tower in the place where a lamp and lens once revolved, throwing light several miles out. The original lantern and Fresnel lens are currently in the Smithsonian Museum in Washington D.C.

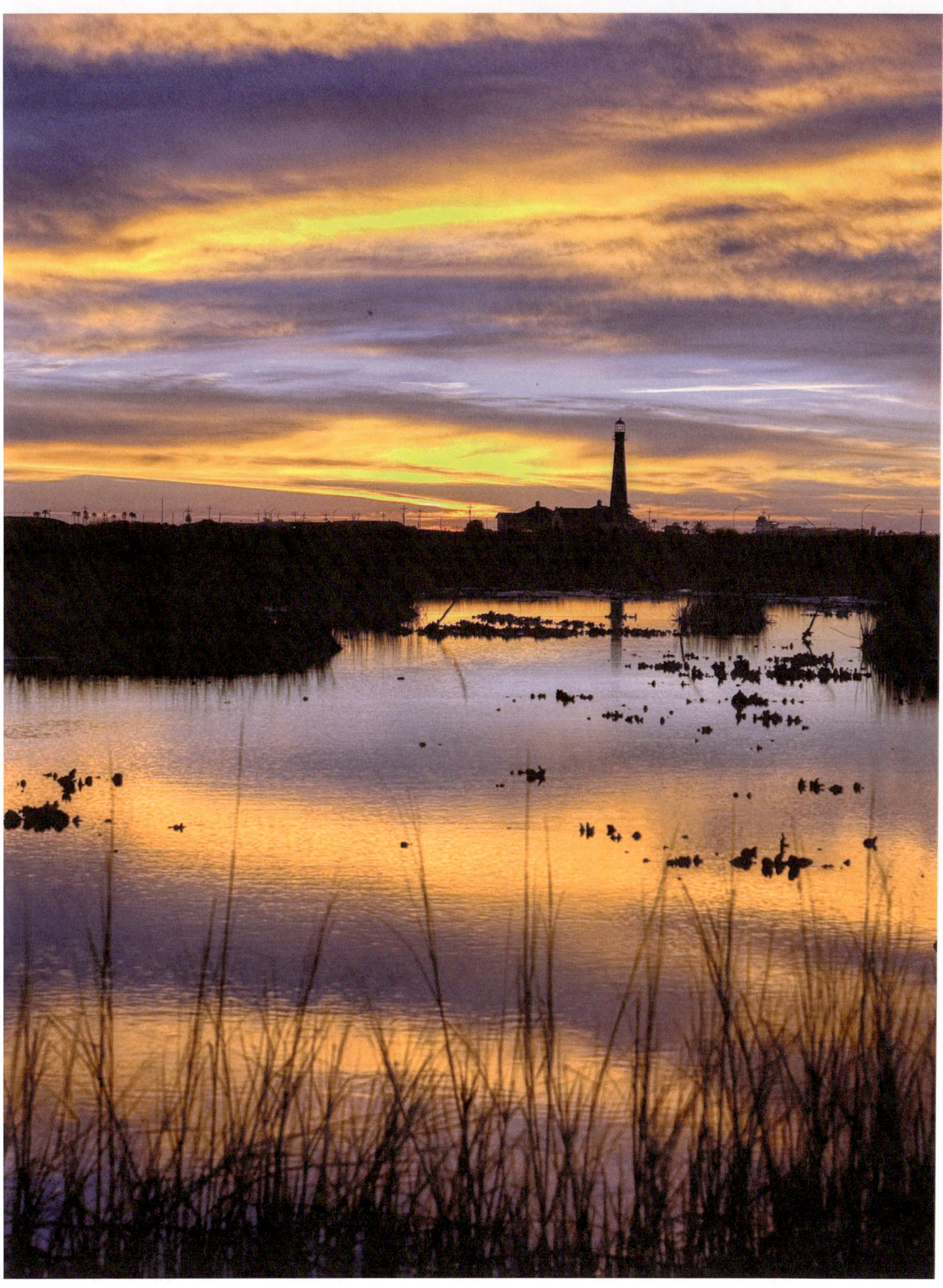

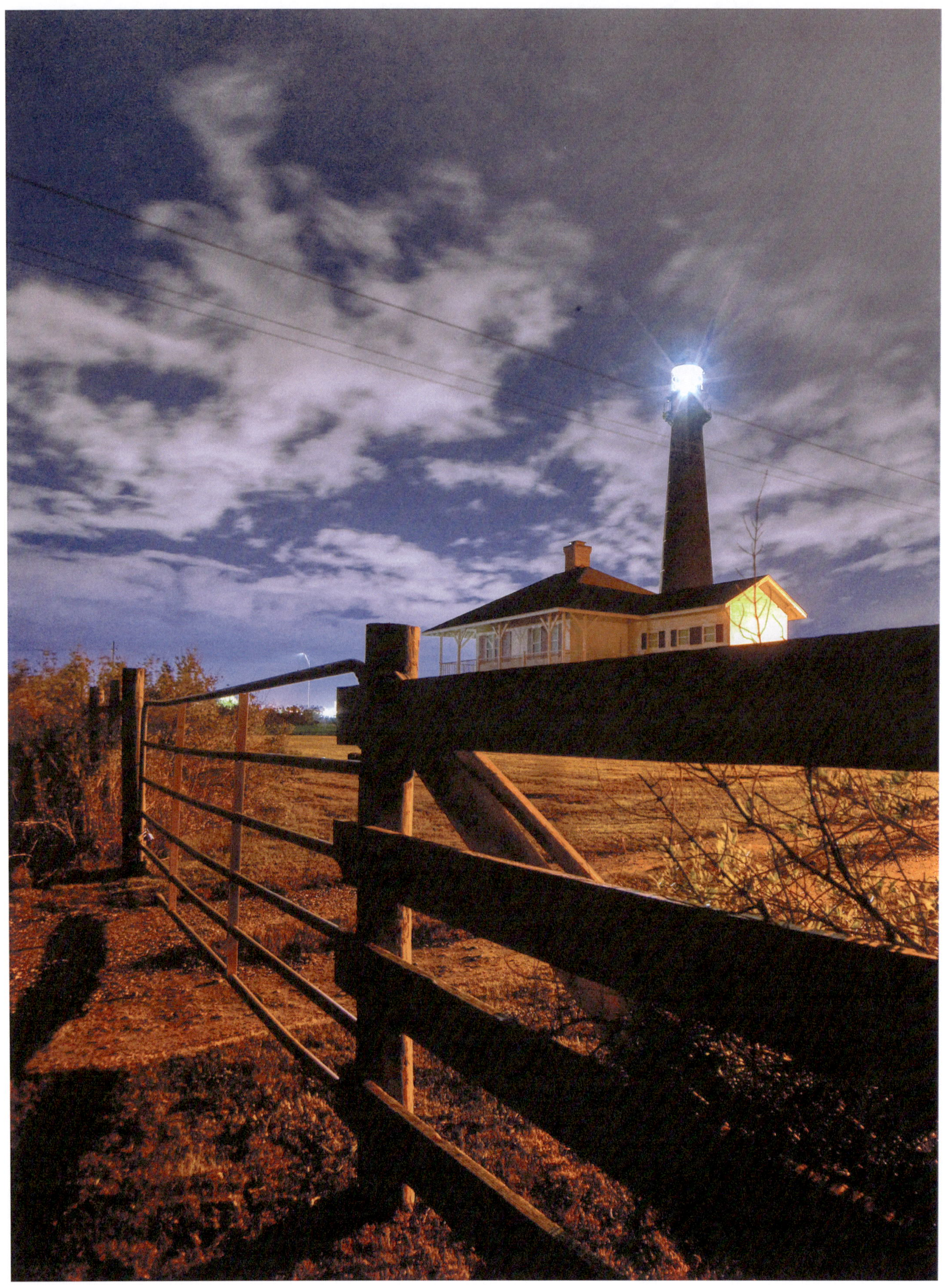

Memories from Don Golden

"I grew up in Beaumont. Bolivar, with its beaches, was a little over an hour's drive away. We were friends with the Maxwells who actually had a beach house in Bolivar. Somehow the Maxwells were connected to the family who lived in the lighthouse caretakers house.

Once or twice each season we spent the weekend with the Maxwells at their beach house. Typically during the weekend, we would all go visit the folks at the light house. There were three or four of us, 6-8 years old, and we'd climb the lighthouse stairs up to the platform at the top.

From the platform, we could take in the amazing view. The Bolivar ferry terminal was the biggest attraction with Galveston in the background.

The Texas city refineries were often visible with ships plying the ship channel in the foreground. The barges in the intercoastal canal were another feature.

Toward the southeast, we could see the hill that marked Fort Travis. Fort Travis and its companion, Fort Crocket on Galveston, guarded the approaches to the Houston ship channel during WWII. Interestingly, the huge naval guns were still there when I was a kid and the fort was accessible so we could check them out.

My dad explained that the forts were there to defend against the German U-boats. The U-boats lurked offshore waiting for cargo ships to depart Galveston enroute to Africa or Europe. The US military manned these forts with their naval rifles trying to sink the subs. I don't know if they ever sank any of them but maybe they deterred them.

Sunsets from the lighthouse were spectacular although that wasn't such a big deal for an eight-year old.

Looking into the compartment at the top of the lighthouse, the huge Fresnell lens dominated the chamber. The mechanism that rotated the light was visible but I don't recall ever seeing it run.

Our biggest adventure was to light firecrackers and drop them from the platform. They almost always exploded in mid air. If we didn't have firecrackers, lit matches were a poor alternative.

I had no idea what a blessing it was to get to know the lighthouse in the 50's."

    - Don Golden, age 75

> "I had no idea what a blessing it was to get to know the lighthouse in the 50's."

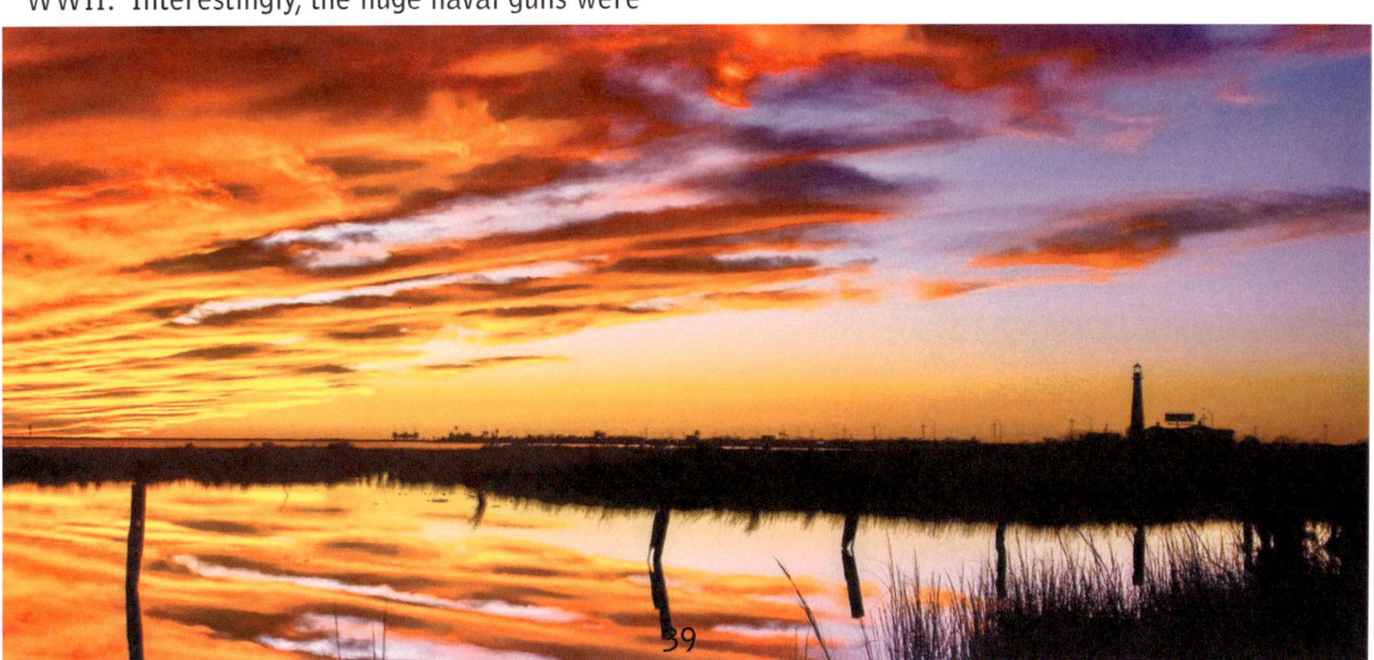

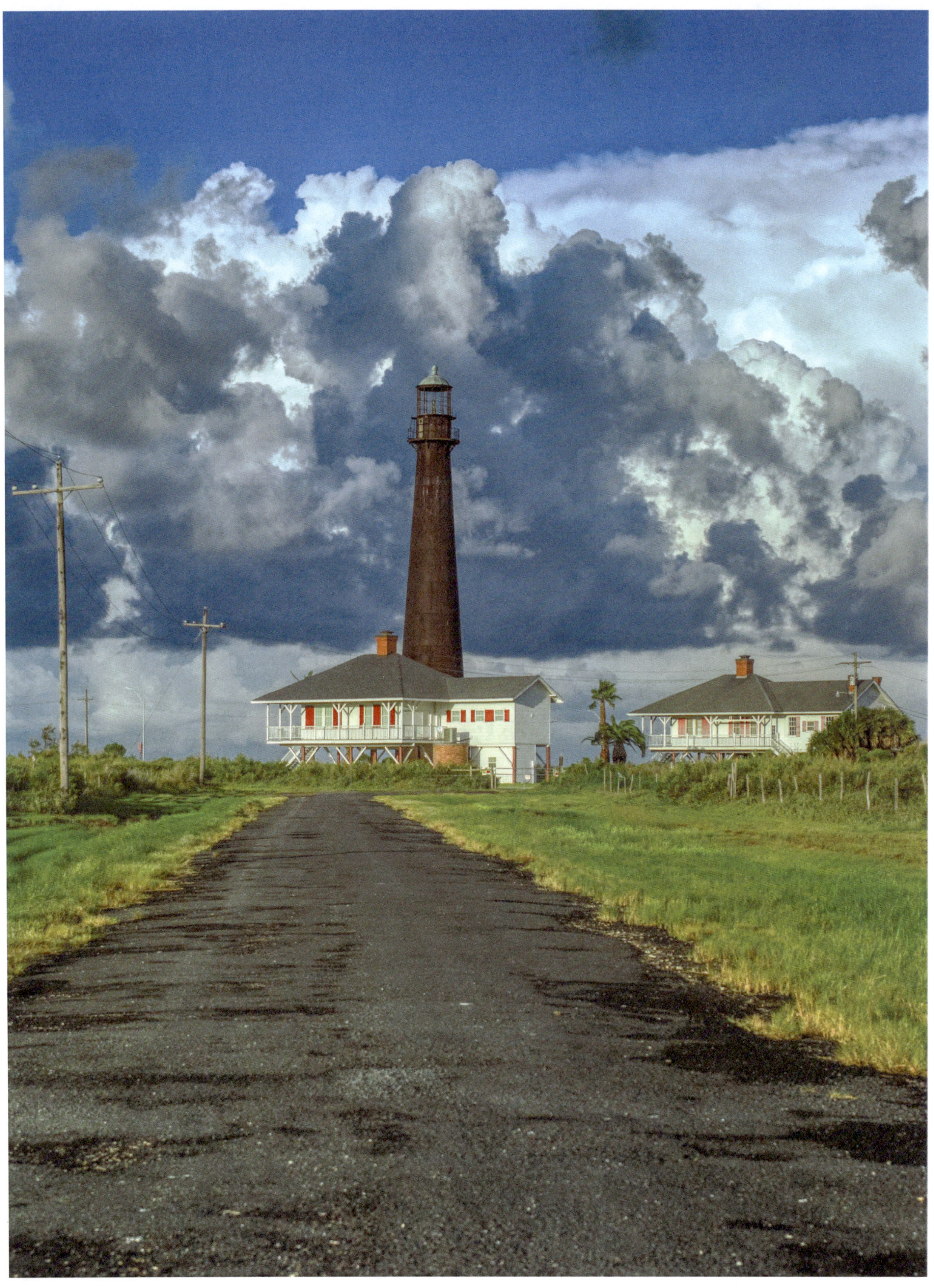

Memories from Pete Chase

"Looking at the lighthouse, you will notice windows vertically aligned with the front door rising up about every 20 feet. These are not only windows bringing in light but also act as vents to bring fresh air inside the stairwell.

At the top of the stairwell, there are about 16 round port windows that allow the air to escape, creating a sort of vacuum within the lighthouse for fresh air. It's common to see these on lighthouses and probably serves other purposes besides the fresh air intake, but without it, the interior would be miserable climbing to the top in the Texas heat.

Since these windows do not have a door mechanism to close them off, I'm sure they create a huge pressure variant and noise issue during an intense wind event like a hurricane.

One feature the designers probably didn't realize back in the late 1800's was the height of the storm surge on Bolivar. One of the windows on the north side facing away from the water is only about six feet off of the ground. This six-foot window opening would be below the storm surge height during any close hurricane which would be a point of water entry.

I don't know the height of the storm surge during the 1900 or 1915 hurricanes, but during Ike in 2008, we estimate the water height was 12 feet at the lighthouse.

Hurricane Ike 2008 was a hold-our-breath moment. Sure, the Bolivar Lighthouse had weathered many storms but she was now 136 years old and there was a massive storm bearing straight toward her.

I remember sitting up most of the night watching the news from Galveston reporting on the storm and seeing the winds picking up and just praying she could manage the winds and storm surge.

Our twin girls were just a couple of weeks old, so that made it easy to stay up since we had to feed them every hour or so. I remember switching back and forth from each news station to see who had live feeds from Galveston.

The next day, there wasn't much news about the Bolivar Peninsula until someone flew a couple of helicopters and small planes to survey the damage. Rows of houses were gone that had been there for many many years, and it was hard to distinguish what streets you were seeing.

There was only one yellow house in Gilchrist standing when there used to be many more, half the bridge at Rollover was destroyed and houses that once were along the beach were now in the bay.

It didn't look good until we happened to see a photo someone took from their plane and posted on the internet. The lighthouse was still standing, the keepers' dwellings were still standing but the water from the gulf and the bay were one.

It would be several weeks before an on-the-ground survey could be done to see what damage was sustained. She did well but she did take damage. Some of the upper sidewalk cracked, the brick oil storage building crashed and some of the masonry was damaged.

Through the years after Ike, more and more pieces have come apart which is of great concern but thankfully the Bolivar Point Lighthouse Foundation has been formed to take on the restoration process to give her another 150 years of life."

- Pete Chase

She's stood tall and strong for 150 years

"Today the white and black painted bands are gone, and she has turned dark brown from the salt air, but she stands for the history of the Bolivar Peninsula, the history of Texas and the history of The United States Marine Commerce that wouldn't have succeeded without lighthouses guiding sailors day and night.

She is the first thing you see landing on the Bolivar Peninsula from the ferry and the last thing you see leaving the peninsula. It is not uncommon to see hundreds of people taking photographs of the lighthouse throughout the day.

We love watching people pull out their cameras while waiting in the ferry line take pictures of the lighthouse. She is beautiful and has stood tall and strong for 150 years on the Texas Coast.

I don't know of a single lighthouse anywhere in the world with so much history. Lighthouses save countless ships but how many have saved hundreds of lives?

I have talked with people that have told me their relatives were some of the survivors who rode out the 1900 and 1915 storms in the lighthouse and that's when they realize they wouldn't be here today if it wouldn't have been for the lighthouse.

If their great great grandparents hadn't been taken to the lighthouse when they were a child to ride the storm out, they wouldn't have made it and they wouldn't be here today."

- Pete Chase

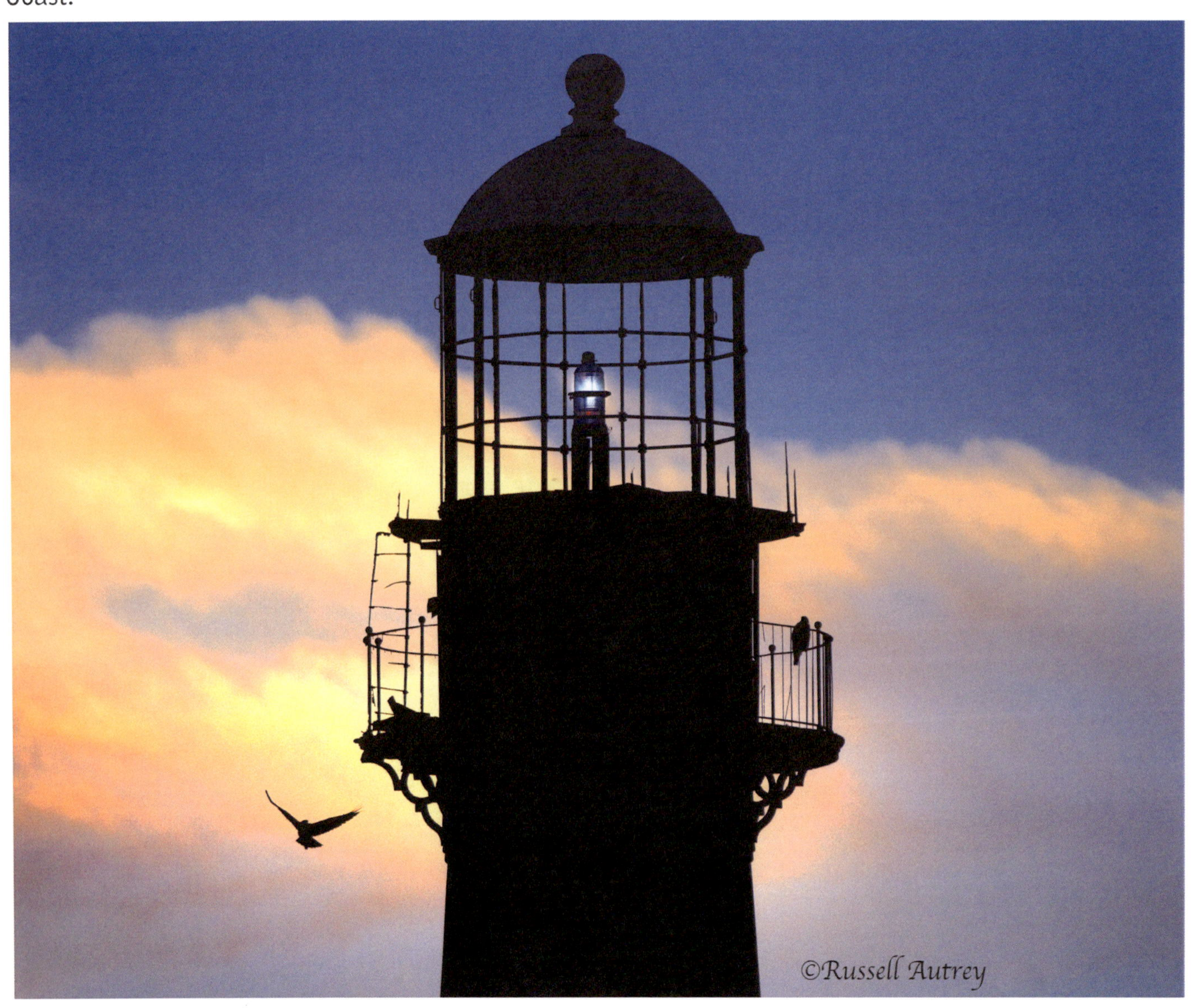

Memories from Michael Maxwell

"I lived in the lighthouse keeper's house from 2000 to 2008 when I was displaced by Hurricane Ike. It was a wonderful experience. I felt blessed the entire time I was there. It took a lot of work to get the house back into good condition, but it was a labor of love for sure. I loved the house, even the mosquitoes.

People would often stop by if I was working outside. I had a little nickel-spiel I'd give them. I knew the specifics of the structure and I'd tell them a brief history. Most people were extremely happy with that. I enjoyed conveying it and hearing their memories of the beach and the lighthouse.

As a child, we used to go to the beach and we'd always, on the drive there, look for the High Island bridge and see who'd be the first one to see the lighthouse. I used to drag my younger cousin Mark to the house and we'd go with tools and work on things or paint. We probably broke more than we fixed, but I had a passion. I wanted to get things back to their specific condition on the house. The lighthouse was too big of a project when we were that age. We'd sweep it out and take friends to the top.

The lighthouse has always been close to my heart. I'd go as often as I could. When I got the opportunity to live there, I took it. I was ecstatic. I worked in Baytown, which was a horrible commute, but I enjoyed living there. Something calls me to that place to keep it up forever."

> "I was always so thankful to be there, watching the sunrise and the sunset from the front porch, just the ambiance of the whole property. I've loved it ever since I can remember."

- Michael Maxwell

Explosions and Cannon Fire

The lighthouse was once fired on accidentally by the U.S. Army. All the glass was blown out in a tragic explosion in Texas City in 1947.

• On April 16, 1947 in Texas City, the freighter Grandcamp was being loaded with ammonium nitrate that was used to create explosives for mining. Smoke was spotted deep within the freighter's holding areas, and the ship exploded. The 1.5-ton anchor was found two miles away, and houses and ships in the area were destroyed. The glass at the top of the Bolivar Lighthouse was smashed by the sound wave from the explosion. In all, 581 people died and over 3,500 people were injured in the blast.

• The lighthouse was decommissioned in 1933. The U.S. Army was on the peninsula and soldiers firing cannons. There's a patch on the outside and the inside of the lighthouse where a cannon shell actually punched a hole through the panel. According to Pete Chase, where the cannon hit the lighthouse looks like a scar on the outside of the structure, but there's a big plate on the inside where someone patched the hole. He said the lighthouse keeper kept radioing for the Army to stop, telling them they were aiming the wrong way.

- Information courtesy of Pete Chase and This Day In History.

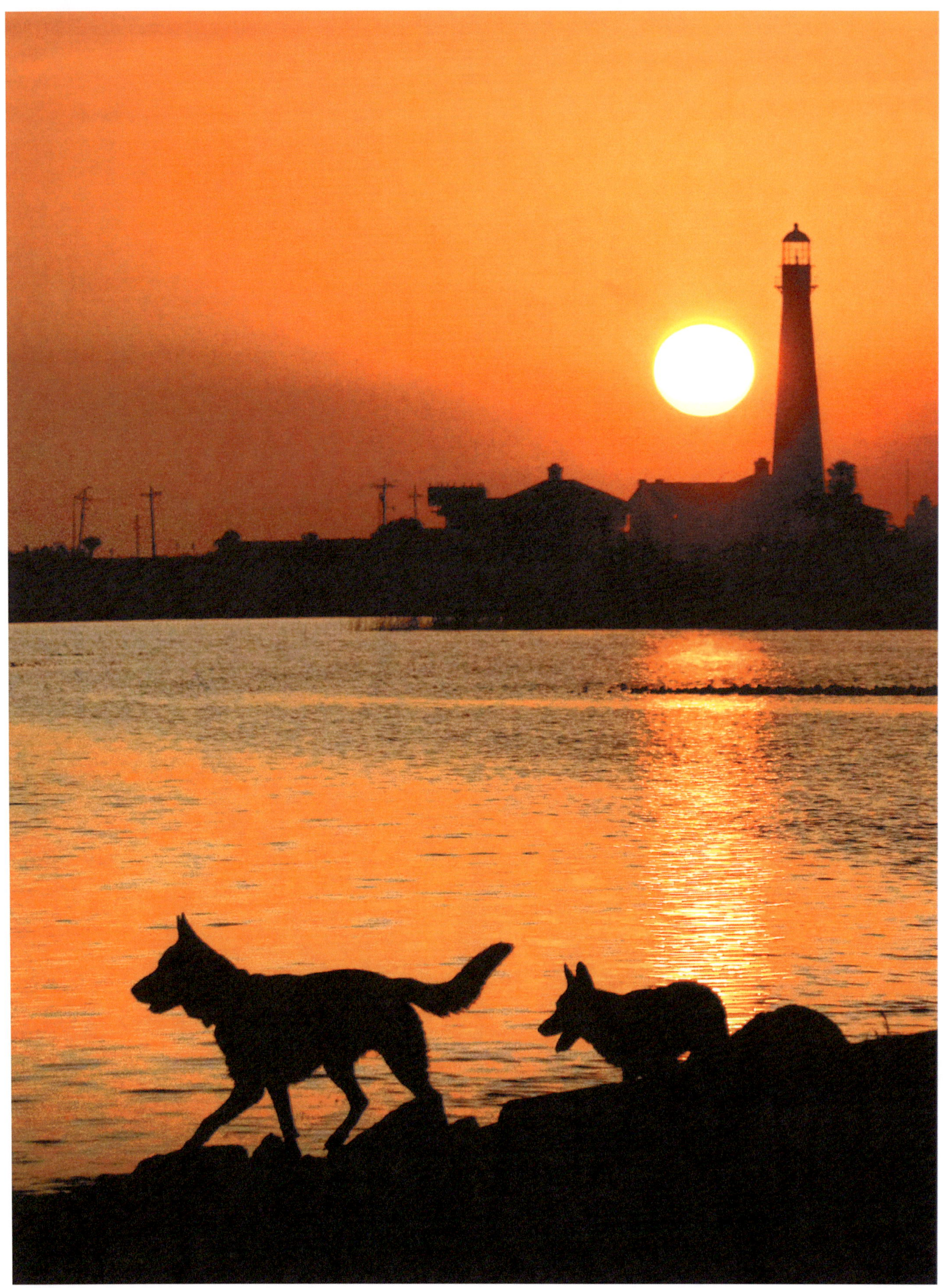

The Texas City Explosion

Lloyd Maxwell, 82, recalled the day the Texas City explosion happened, April 16, 1947. Buildings were destroyed and an anchor from one of the ships was found miles away. Overall, the death toll was more than 500 people. This is Mr. Maxwell's memory of that time:

"Texas City is about eight miles as the crow flies from the Bolivar Lighthouse across the water to the west.

The heat from the fire burned all the paint off of the west side of both of the beach houses. They had to be repainted, and they had to replace the windows because the concussion blew the windows out. The explosion knocked a lot of the bricks loose inside the lighthouse so there had to be some repair work done in the lighthouse.

When Texas City blew up, we lived in Devers, Texas. That's between Liberty and Beaumont. The explosion from the Grand Camp, the big ship, broke the widows in the Devers school.

Some people say it looked like a mushroom cloud but it looked like a big thunderhead to us. We heard what happened on the radio. Within a matter of six to seven hours of that explosion, we noticed all these ambulances and fire trucks coming past our house. Most were military as this was after World War II. They came in for three to four days from the east.

The only way to get to Texas City was to come down Highway 90. That's where all the ambulances and fire trucks were going. That was a vivid recollection. All five of us boys remembered that quite well.

I went to high school with a boy from Liberty, Joe Blackburn, and he was playing football with David. We noticed that Joe had a lot of scars on his back. Come to find out, Joe's family lived in Texas City and his dad worked in the refinery. When the first ship started exploding, his daddy loaded up him and his mama in the car.

They decided to leave, and when they got about two miles out of town, the Grand Camp ship blew up, the big one, and a piece of plate steel from the side of that ship went through the roof of their car and killed his parents and he was in the back seat. He had terrible burns all over his back. That was about two miles away from the explosion."

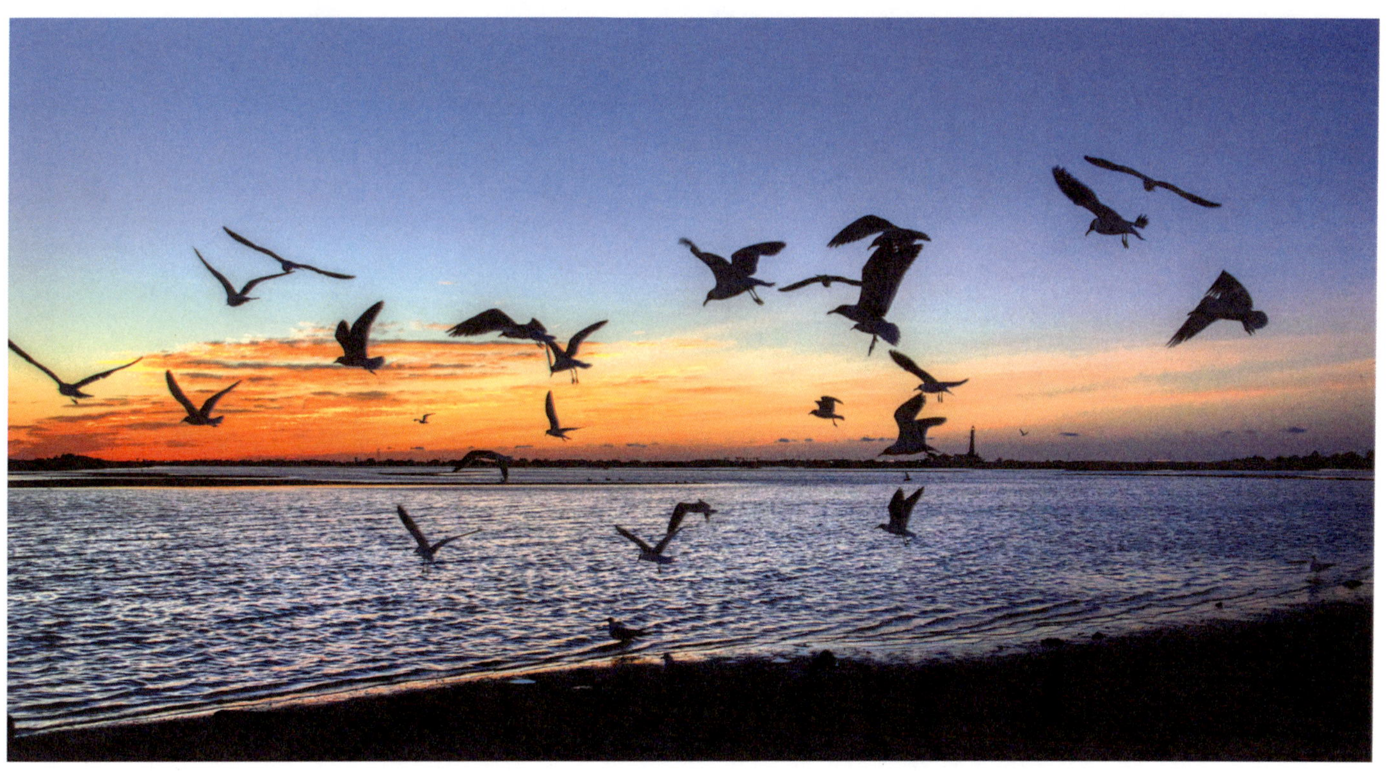

"I bought a telephoto lens to watch ships passing by in the day and night. After a few days, my attention turned to birds and the beauty of nature. And what better place to retire for a photographer than one with a view of a lighthouse .

I began documenting the birds and wildlife in the Audubon Horseshoe Marsh Bird Sanctuary as well as photographing the fascinating iron tower and soon became friends wuth the Chase family. Pete is the historian while Amy is a descendant of the original buyer of the lighthouse when it was sold to Elmer Boyt and is the Executive Director of the Bolivar Point Lighthouse Foundation."

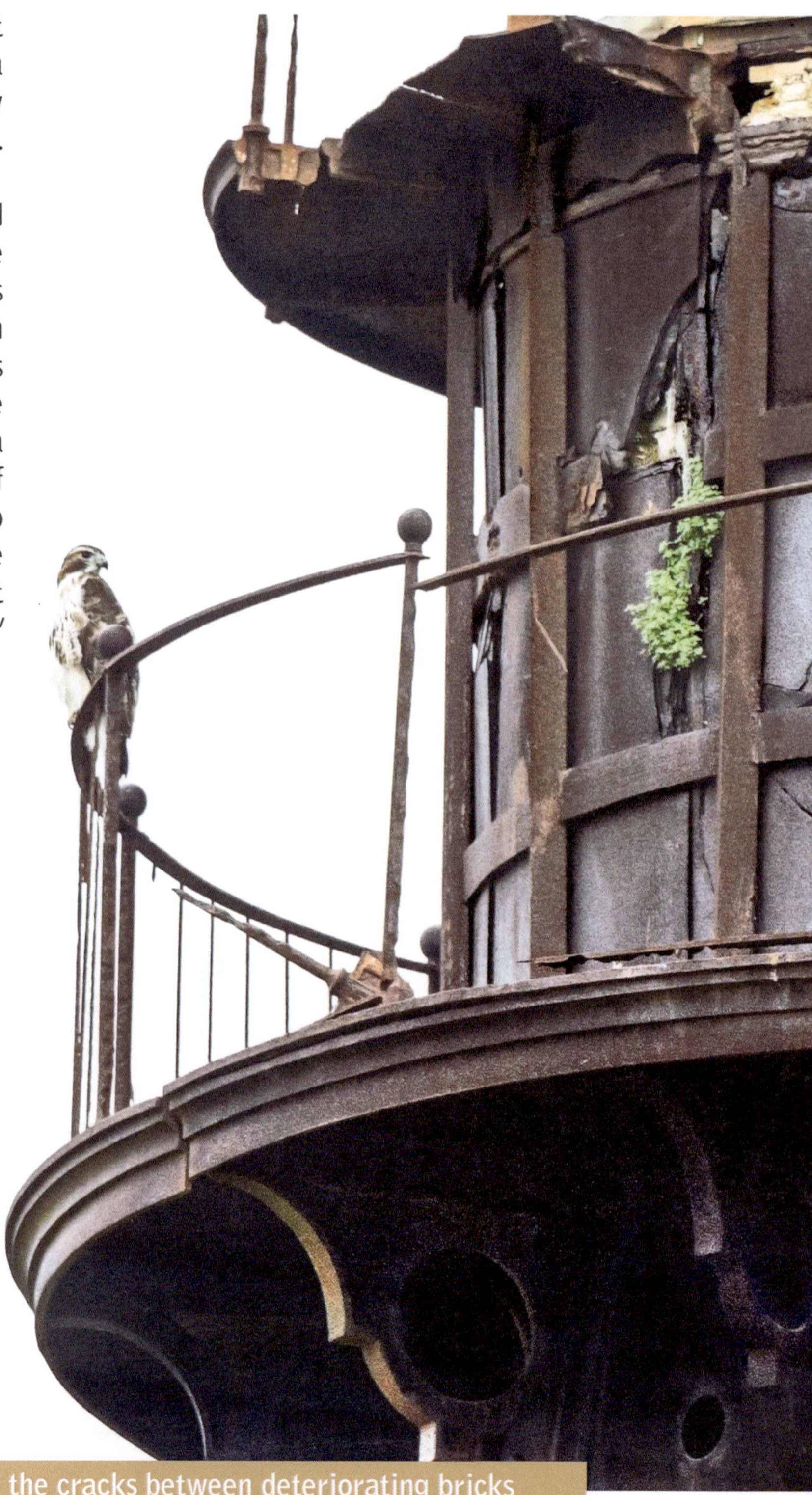

Green vines grow in the cracks between deteriorating bricks and cracked iron plates near the top where a mechanical room once housed gears for turning the revolving beam of light. During the 1915 storm, the lighthouse keeper turned the beam manually when the mechanism failed.

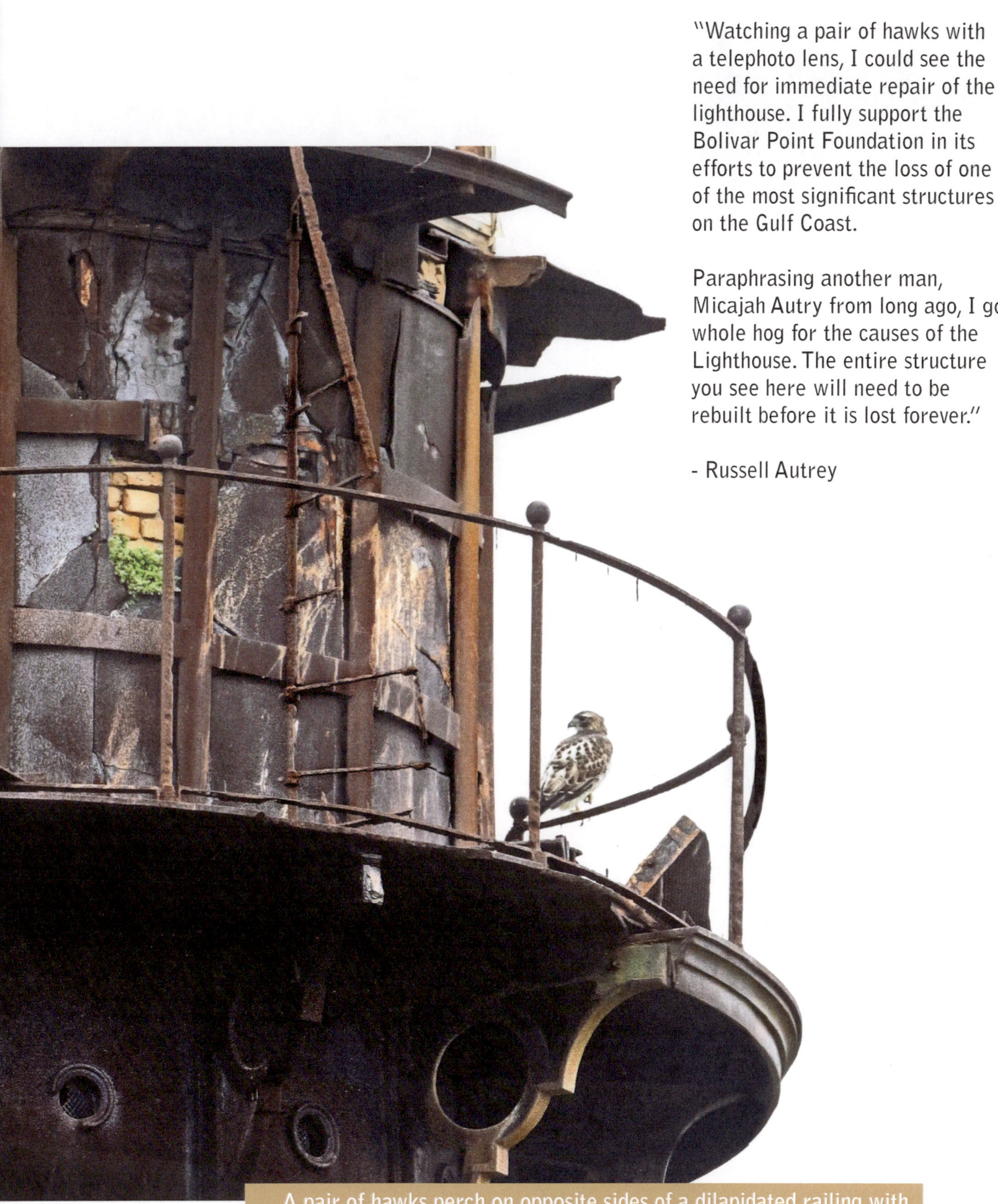

"Watching a pair of hawks with a telephoto lens, I could see the need for immediate repair of the lighthouse. I fully support the Bolivar Point Foundation in its efforts to prevent the loss of one of the most significant structures on the Gulf Coast.

Paraphrasing another man, Micajah Autry from long ago, I go whole hog for the causes of the Lighthouse. The entire structure you see here will need to be rebuilt before it is lost forever."

- Russell Autrey

A pair of hawks perch on opposite sides of a dilapidated railing with most of the balusters missing. The walkway encircling the tower allowed access by the twisted rusted ladder above to a small ledge from where the windows could be washed that shielded the kerosene-fueled lamp from the weather.

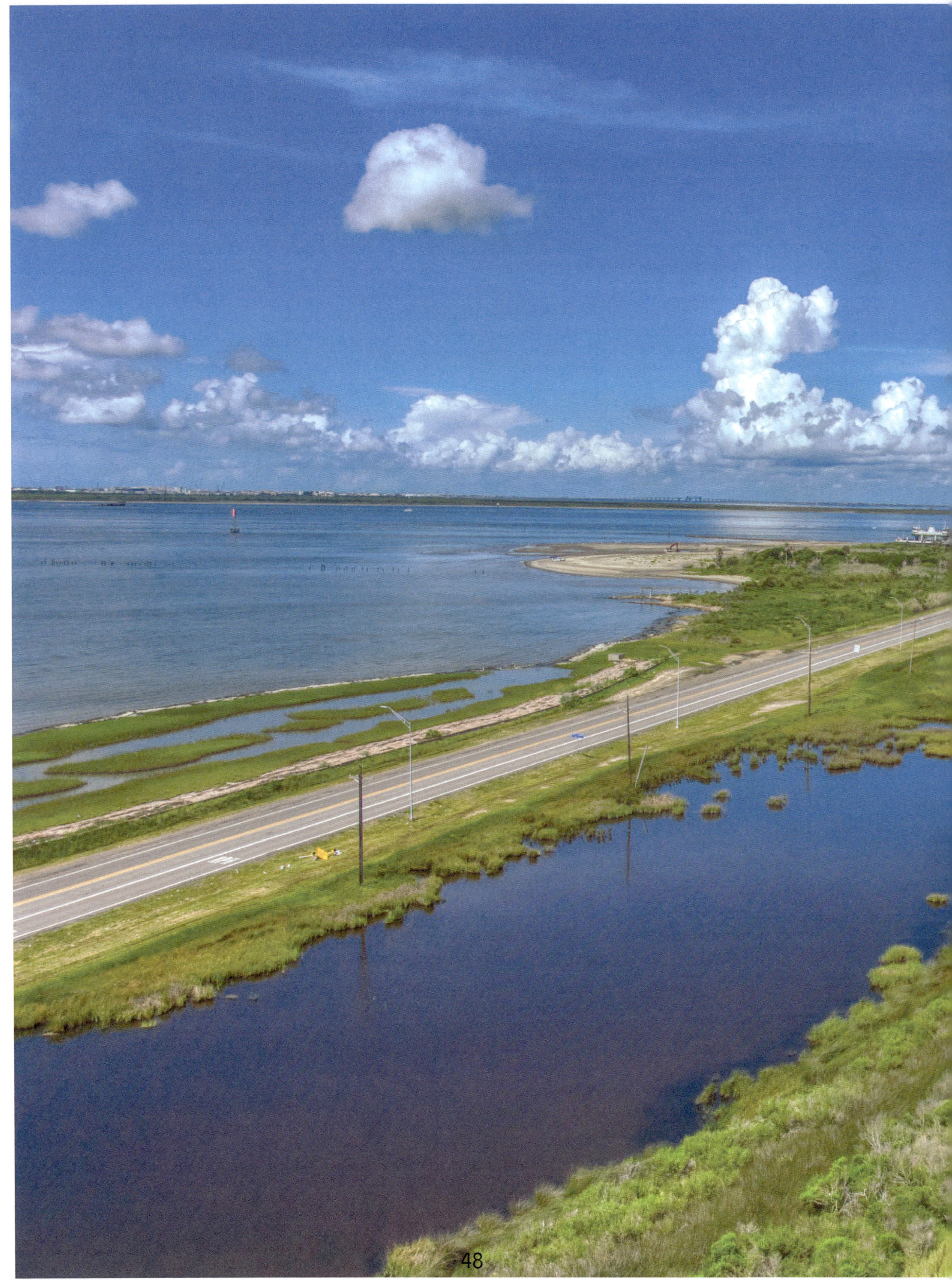

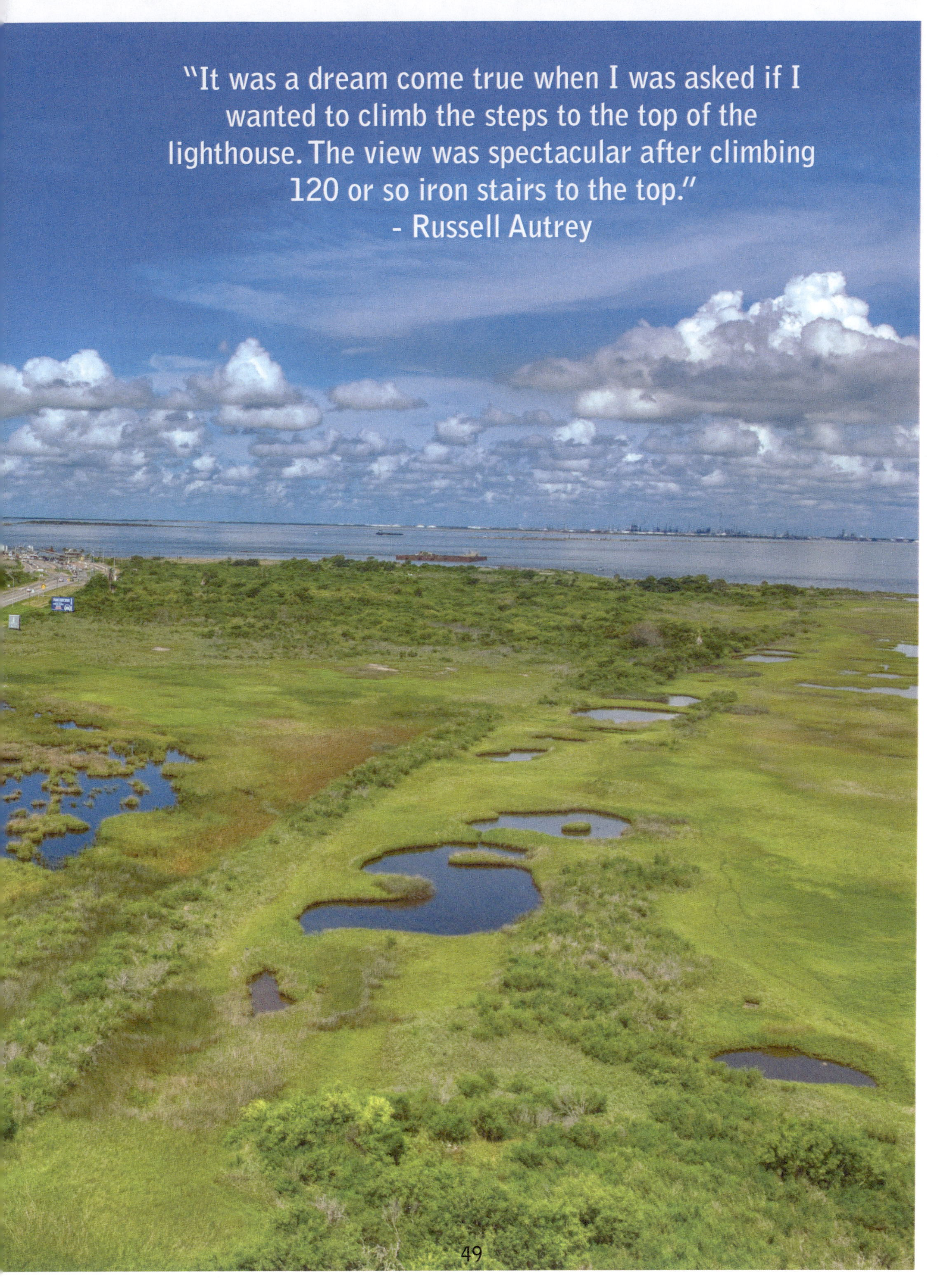
"It was a dream come true when I was asked if I
wanted to climb the steps to the top of the
lighthouse. The view was spectacular after climbing
120 or so iron stairs to the top."
- Russell Autrey

Acknowledgements

The authors would like to thank those who shared their memories, photos and family memorabilia of the lighthouse and growing up on Bolivar Peninsula.

These storytellers include Linda Adams, Kathy Autrey, Robert Bouse, Amy Boyt Maxwell, Mark Boyt, Pete Chase, Sylvia Comeaux, Don Golden, Randall Harrington, Mark Kelso, Rita and George Lind, Michael Maxwell, Kay McCowen Laudig, Elle Whittington and Alleen Williams.

They would also like to thank the Maxwell and Boyt families for their time and generosity in sharing family stories and memories. They'd also like to thank Hal Schmidt for his technical expertise. The writers and contributors regret any errors as they are unintentional.

Send donations toward restoration of the lighthouse to: Bolivar Point Lighthouse Foundation, P. O. Box 385, Port Bolivar, TX 77650. The foundation thanks you for your interest and generosity.

"I'd definitely like to see the lighthouse restored. It's going to be 150 years old in 2022.

There's a lot of history there. So many people would drive down and talk to us about their grandparents who survived in the 1900 and 1915 storms.

If they hadn't survived in the lighthouse, we wouldn't be here."

- Lloyd Maxwell, age 82

The publisher and authors have made every effort to ensure that the information in this book was correct at press time. While this publication is designed to provide accurate information in regard to the subject matter covered, the publisher and the author assume no responsibility for errors, inaccuracies, omissions, or any other inconsistencies herein and hereby disclaim any liability to any party for any loss, damage, or disruption caused by errors or omissions, whether such errors or omissions result from negligence, accident, or any other cause. This publication is meant as a source of valuable information for the reader; however, it is not meant as a substitute for direct expert assistance. If such level of assistance is required, the services of a competent professional should be sought.

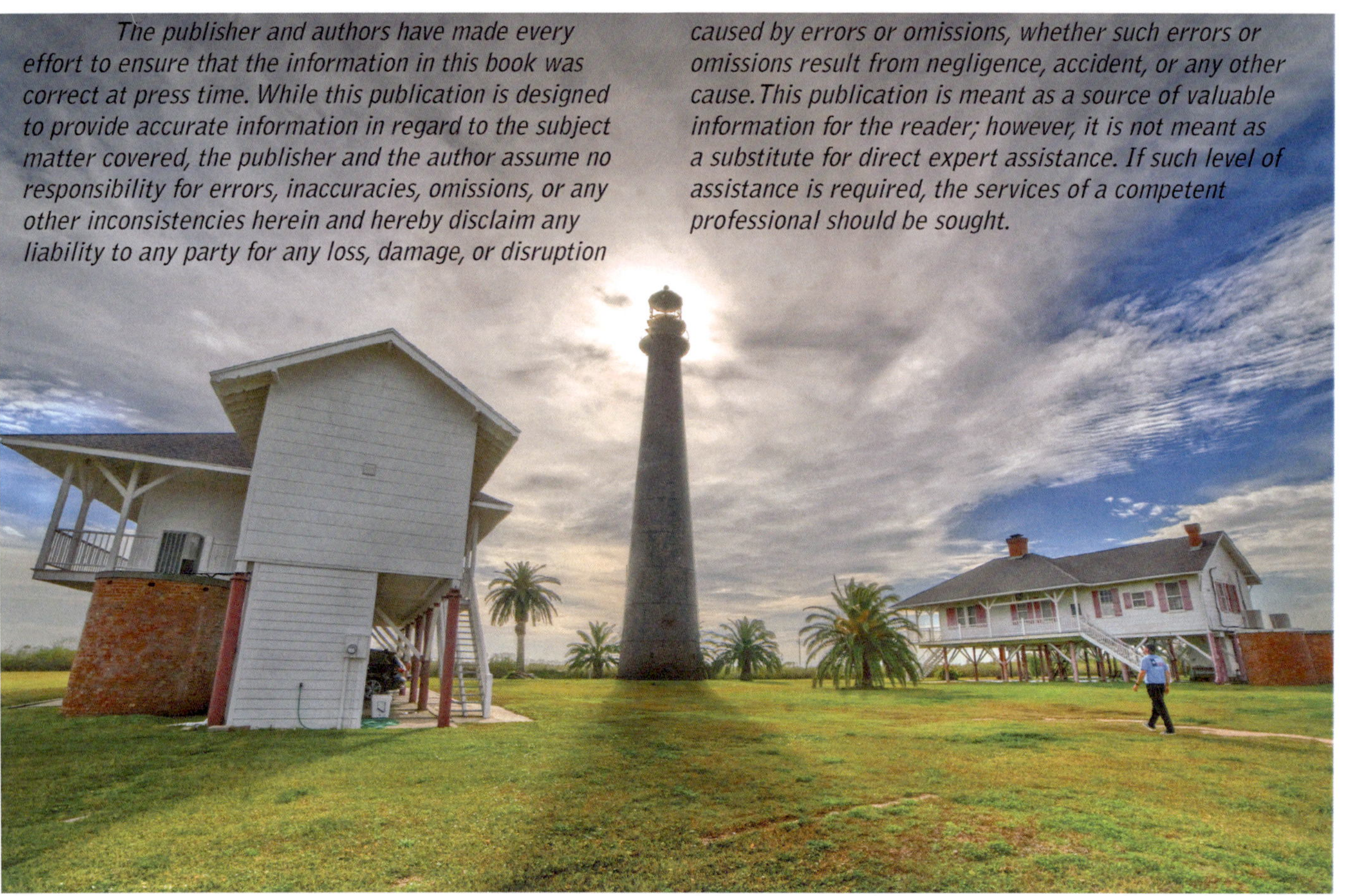

CPSIA information can be obtained
at www.ICGtesting.com
Printed in the USA
BVRC100941040322
629736BV00009B/4

9 781736 313008